Larry —
Enjoy some
Texas golf
history!

When Golf Was Fun

Pat

WHEN GOLF WAS FUN
Tales from the Late, Great Beer and Barbecue Circuit

Pat Wheeler

When Golf was Fun: Tales from the Late, Great Beer and Barbecue Circuit

Author: Pat Wheeler

Published by Austin Brothers Publishing
Keller, Texas
www.austinbrotherspublishing.com

ISBN 978-0-9853263-4-0

Cover Design by Jeff Austin
Cover photo provided by *DFW Link*s magazine

This and other books published by Austin Brothers Publishing can be purchased at www.austinbrotherspublishing.com.

Printed in the United States of America

2012 -- First Edition

For Mom, Dad, Mike, and Tim

Contents

"He lifted me out of the slimy pit, out of the mud and the mire; he set my feet on a rock and gave me a firm place to stand."

Psalm 40:2

Acknowledgments

I want to thank my family and friends who encouraged me to finish this book. The nucleus of the material first appeared in a four-part series in both *DFW Links* and *Houston Links* magazines during the summer and fall of 2010. A special debt of gratitude is owed to the publisher of those magazines, Kevin Newberry, for giving me the opportunity to write for his publications. I have learned a great deal from his encouragement and constructive criticism.

This book just skims the surface of the great golf stories from the old beer and barbecue circuit. I know I have left out some great players and great stories. Please forgive me for any glaring omissions or stories that you find offensive. This was written in the spirit of remembering the fun times of the past.

There are two other men who deserve special mention. I want to thank Terry Austin for his help in editing and composing the manuscript and David Glover, a longtime friend and mentor, for providing a final push to help me complete the project.

Above all else, golf is meant to be fun. That is what hooked most of us in the beginning and should keep us coming back for more. Because it is such a difficult game, golf seems to attract and develop unique personalities. Those interesting and entertaining people are the heart and soul of this book.

Most of all, this book would never have been written but for the grace of a loving God and my Savior, Jesus Christ.

Foreword

By Kevin Newberry

It was a much simpler time.

There were no GPS systems or range finders to give you exact yardage to the hole. There was no *Golf Channel* with 24/7 infomercials with swing advice and quick fixes. There were no sports psychologists to tell you how to think your way around the course. There were no video cameras with frame-by-frame slow-motion to record and analyze your swing. There were no machines to measure your swing speed or match you with the right kind of ball, the right kind of shaft, or club head.

There was a fledgling tour still part of the PGA of America but certainly no American Junior Golf Association to promote the game's promising young players.

The golf courses were hardscrabble, where it was often impossible to tell the difference between the fairway and rough. In many cases, fairways and roughs were simply closely cropped hardpan.

As golf history goes, it wasn't really that long ago. But in the 1940s, the golf world was still much like the Wild West before it gave way to the Industrial Age. Golf's post-Depression era was full of larger than life characters with larger than life stories that are just too far-fetched to possibly make up.

Golf was still a game back then, not an industry.

People who loved the game were still trying to figure out how to make a living at it. Even in the early days of the pro tour, pros lived a vagabond existence from one town to the next trying to string together four good rounds to win a top prize of maybe $2,000 (minus expenses), all while holding down a full-time job as a club pro somewhere.

To many great golfers, the pro tour wasn't all that attractive.

Welcome to the late, great beer and barbecue circuit, a bygone era of Texas golf in which many Lone Star legends were born and raised but has since given way to the more civilized and organized golf industry we know today. Much like baseball's barnstorming days, the barbecue circuit was a series of unaffiliated events that brought an extremely high level of golf and excitement to tiny towns like Center and Athens; Quanah and Pampa— places you might otherwise never have known even existed.

There were different circuits in East Texas, West Texas and South Texas. In each town, it was the social event of the year. Townspeople would open up their homes for the chance to house one of the game's legends for a few days. Even little old ladies sometimes saved up their money all year to buy a player in the Calcutta.

Since golf was still loosely organized at most levels, these events were the only way for most golfers to match their skills against the game's other best players. So the entrants included an interesting assortment of people and personalities–from youngsters trying to get noticed for a scholarship, to college hot shots cutting their teeth in preparation for a pro career, to career amateurs still capable of beating the best pros on their local course. Some were even professional hustlers who always played just well enough to win or maybe even intentionally lost if their bets were right.

These players didn't worry about high fashion as most played in T-shirts and many didn't even have a matched set of clubs. But they sure as heck could golf their ball.

What was the draw to these tiny Texas towns?

First, it was the competition. It meant something to win one of these things. It served as a gauge for how far you could go in this game. Secondly, it was the money. While these tournaments did not have official *purses* like modern-day golf, amateur golfers who were purchased in the Calcutta by other players or onlookers would often get a piece of the action if they won. Of course, it was all under the table, unofficial. They would get an envelope or a shoebox full of money on the way to the parking lot. It was how many college players from modest backgrounds earned spending money during their college days.

In the early 1980s, things got so big that the Calcutta pool at the Center Invitational, considered by many to be the Granddaddy of all barbecue circuit events, reached $112,000. The winning buyer might get $40,000 and the winning player might get $4,000 of that action.

That's when the NCAA and USGA, which had turned a blind eye for more than four decades, decided to crack down on amateur participation in these events. After all, accepting money was a violation of the rules of amateur status. That crackdown hastened the end of one of the most colorful eras in Texas golf history.

Many of those guys eventually turned pro anyway. Who were they? Well, from the early days of the barbecue circuit there was Miller Barber, Don January, Billy Maxwell, and Earl Stewart. They were followed by the likes of Charles Coody and Jacky Cupit, who gave way to Ben Crenshaw and Bruce Lietzke and finally to the generation that included Mark Brooks and Hal Sutton.

And that's not to mention the countless colorful characters that you never heard of, including notorious golfer/gambler Dick Martin, who always said he couldn't afford to turn pro. He died a multi-millionaire.

Preface

"We can't all be Mark Twain, so write about what you like."

Herbert Warren Wind

Bedford, Massachusetts

It was one of those eerie afternoons in a North Texas autumn when a thunderstorm is looming. You know it's going to rain but just not sure when. It was about mid-morning on a Saturday when I rang the doorbell at the home of Bill Hooton.

He cordially invited me back to his patio that overlooked a gold fish pond in the heart of Highland Park on Turtle Creek Avenue. To get there, we walked through his library that was full of golf and history books. We had the most pleasant of conversations about everything from the Premier golf course to him playing basketball against Jacky Cupit when Jacky was at Pine Tree High School and Bill at Pittsburg High School.

The name Tommy Minter even came up, which I had not heard for many years. I immediately recalled what a great track star he was and at that Bill led me back into his library to show me one of his many well-kept scrap books. In one of them was Tommy Minter in high school when he scored enough points to win the district championship by himself. He was a Gladewater Bear and of course became a track and football star later as a Baylor Bear. That was in the early 1960s.

It was Bill Hooton who called me out of the blue and encouraged me to continue writing articles about the old beer and barbecue circuit. He gave me Ben Crenshaw's cell phone number and called Ben to tell him that I was going to give him a call. Bill and Ben had been friends since meeting at the Pavilion Tent at one of the early Byron Nelson tournaments at Preston Trail Golf Club where Bill was a member.

I had a conversation with Ben and he said he had not heard Bill Hooton as excited about anything like he was about the old barbecue golf stories in some time. Ben encouraged me by saying that someone needs to write down some of the stories about the old barbecue tournaments.

Bill and I visited for more than an hour with only a short interruption by his wife to let me know that their daughter had noticed the window down in my rental car and that I had better get it rolled up before the rains hit. That's the kind of people the Hootons are.

We lost Bill about six or so months after our conversation and I didn't want the reader to get into this book without thinking for a moment about Bill Hooton and his fun outlook on life and how much he enjoyed remembering the old barbecue tournaments. He had relationships with people like Ben Crenshaw and George W. Bush.

He recalled a fishing trip with Bush outside of Athens. Early one morning when it was still dark, Bill noticed the light on in Bush's room and inquired if the future president had trouble sleeping sometimes as well. He said that Bush told him that he enjoyed reading early each morning. When Hooton asked what Bush was reading, he was told the Bible. It is comforting to know that a president of the United States has read through the Bible several times.

I cannot thank people enough for their encouragement and sharing their stories of a time most of us recall fondly. In thanking Bill posthumously, I am also thanking each person who took the time to share their memories with me and made this book possible. There is enough material for another volume or two about this subject.

I want to express my condolences to Bill's wife and family and just share one story about his love of golf and sense of humor. It seems Bill had a favorite caddie at Preston Trail who called Bill by a most unflattering nickname. He would even call Bill's house and ask for him by this nickname, which was crude, to put it mildly. Bill's wife would just say, "Honey, I think this call is for you."

One day at the Trail, Bill had a big money putt late in the round. It was about 15 feet long with a lot of break from right to left. Before attempting the putt, Bill asked this same caddie, "What do you think?"

Using his unflattering nickname, the caddie simply said, "I think you're gonna miss it."

Introduction

If you did well, some guy who bought you in the Calcutta would slip you some money.

Joe Black

Austin, Texas

Tall, rangy, supremely confident and successful in the oil business, Leon Taylor of Tyler and Raleigh Selby of Kilgore would climb into the *Texas Bullet*, Taylor's single engine airplane built in Tyler in the 1940s and zoom off into the air in search of a good money game or the next stop on the beer and barbecue circuit. Sidekicks until their final days, it was nothing for Taylor and Selby to land next to a fairway in Corsicana or Odessa.

It was leaving the Odessa Pro-Am one year when the *Texas Bullet* clipped a wire and tumbled to the flat ground of West Texas. Taylor and Kilgore golf pro Red Weidner escaped unharmed but perhaps a little rattled and the resilient aircraft had to be towed back to Tyler.

Such were the glorious early days of the Texas beer and barbecue circuit where every little town had a big

The Texas Bullet

tournament for one week each year. The stories of great golf attest to the compelling nature of the competition during this era of amateur golf.

A young boy caddying at the Pinecrest Invitational in Longview burst into tears and began rolling around on the green because his older brother lost in sudden death to a guy who would go on to win the British Amateur. The crying young boy would grow up to win the Canadian Open as his same big brother finished second. Two years later he lipped out a putt that would have won the U.S. Open on the 72nd hole at the same course that Francis Ouimet put American golf on the map a half century earlier.

The year was 1948 and the boy was Jacky Cupit. It was Joe Conrad, only 18, who defeated a 21-year-old Buster Cupit that day. Seven years later, Conrad, an up and coming amateur from San Antonio, played on a winning Walker Cup team at St. Andrews and then won the British Amateur in England at Royal Lytham and St. Annes.

The younger Cupit's fateful putt that cost him a U.S. Open was at The Country Club in Brookline, Massachusetts, in 1963. He lost in a playoff the next day to Julius Boros with Arnold Palmer the third player in that match.

Another young boy spent the night sleeping in a sand trap at Brackenridge Park in San Antonio during the state junior tournament that same year. He and his friend from Lamesa sold their return bus tickets so they could get something to eat. They hitchhiked home the next day and thought nothing of it. That young boy was Joe Black, who later worked his way to the top of his profession as president of the PGA of America and is best known as a rules authority and the architect of the split between the PGA Tour and the PGA of America that has served both organizations well.

Speaking about the barbecue tournaments, Joe Black said:

I think it is a shame that they are not played anymore because it was a great training ground for people to play golf. For people like me it was good because at that time, the parents couldn't afford to send you anywhere. So the tournaments were a way to get to play all summer. People would put you up in their homes. They had the barbecue and a dance on Saturday night and then you would win some spending money.

Black remembers the stops as if it were yesterday:

West Texas had a circuit in the summer. Abilene was always the fourth of July and the Odessa pro-am was a big one every summer. They had the Amarillo Partnership at Ross Rogers every year. You played all over. The only one I remember winning was at Eastland.

If you did well, the guy who bought you in the Calcutta would slip you some money. Besides Eastland that I won in 1951 or 1952, I also won one in Ruidoso in 1952. I was working in the pro shop at the Abilene Country Club and some of the members had summer homes there. I beat the New Mexico amateur champion in the finals.

Back in East Texas, the younger Cupit soon grew old enough to win more than his share of the beer and barbecue tournaments. "The thing I remember most is beating Homero Blancas at Center one year because he was the hottest player on the barbecue circuit in those days," Cupit said. "All of the tournaments had good Calcutta pools and were popular. It was customary that whoever won would give you some money under the table. The competition was good."

It was Blancas who shot the historic 55 at the Premier Invitational near Longview in 1962. He is forever known as *Mr. 55*:

Those tournaments were suited for my game because the courses weren't too long, all of them under 7,000 yards. Back then I hit the ball pretty far so I had a lot of wedges to par fours and nothing usually longer than a seven-iron and I could almost reach the par fives and my short game was really good then. I made my share of money in those days. The better you played, the more money you made.

The Calcutta was definitely the drawing card for the top players through the years and often it wasn't the only gambling taking place. Don Cherry was a top amateur player in the 1950s and almost won the 1960 U.S. Open as an amateur at Cherry Hills in Denver. A man of many talents, Cherry still sings professionally but learned his golf on the barbecue circuit of West Texas:

The main reason I went to them was to make money in the Calcutta. An example is one time I went to Brady to play an exhibition with Byron Nelson and found out that they didn't have a Calcutta. So I played the exhibition and then called out to Hobbs, New Mexico and asked if I could still get in their tournament and they said yes. I don't know if you have ever been there but the first hole is a par five and the second hole a par four and the third hole a par five. The first round I go 3-2-3 so that I am six under through three holes. I wind up shooting 60 in the first round and win the tournament. They give me a trophy and the guy in the Calcutta gives me six-hundred dollars. I get talked into a craps game and eight hours later I have lost all of it, the money and the trophy. I go home with nothing. It was something in those days.

A lot of people frowned on such activities, including the USGA, but it was a way of life in small-town Texas for many years.

"It was not a pure, clean deal with some of the things that went on but for the most part the Calcuttas were run fairly," said Black:

The players were auctioned off and when the tournament was over the people put up their money and everyone was pretty much satisfied. If you played good, the guy who bought you would slip you an envelope and you didn't know how much it was. And sometimes a guy wouldn't get what he thought he deserved. Say the guy who bought you made a couple of thousand bucks and gave you $50, that didn't seem right.

In those early days, Calcutta pools were not limited to the Texas beer and barbecue tournaments. One tournament in Georgia had some Calcutta action back in the day. "They had a Calcutta pool with the Masters for years," Black said:

It was not at the club but downtown at the Bon Air Hotel. It was a big time Calcutta tournament. It wasn't conducted by the Augusta National but a lot of the people who were involved with Augusta National were involved with the Calcutta. It was a different time then. There were big money games all over the country then. The rule had been there to a certain degree all along but it wasn't enforced. Then it came to a head and the USGA made an issue out of it and after that was the demise of the Calcutta tournaments.

The quality of play on the beer and barbecue circuit was something to marvel. Bill Holstead won the 1970 Texas State Amateur and has played in seventeen USGA events but his heart still yearns for his early days in Wichita Falls and the West Texas circuit:

The first men's tournament I played in was in 1958 at Pampa. It was a tournament that they called The Top of Texas. It was played Labor Day weekend and I went up there and got beat but I remember watching those good players like Don Massengale and John Paul Cain.

Describing the tournament, Holstead said:

With nine holes to go, I think Don had a three stroke lead and shot a 32. And the legend, the plumber from Lubbock, Roland Adams, shot a 28 and beat him! It was my first introduction to Roland

Adams. Around 1960, no one in the world could beat him in West Texas. And another legend was Jack Williams of Plainview. Those guys played so good. Jack is deceased now but Roland is still living in Lubbock.

Don January fondly remembers playing those desert courses of West Texas:

The courses we learned to play on around here were hard, in that the ground was hard. Especially in West Texas, the only way you could tell the difference between the fairways and the rough was with a line they dug with a one disk plow where everything inside was fairway and everything outside was rough. There wasn't much grass either place. So you didn't have to be long, just get it going straight and it would roll about 150 yards. But the greens were nice. They were beautiful.

The 1967 winner of the PGA Championship and a dominant force on the Champions Tour in the early 1980s, January enjoyed his days of amateur golf on the barbecue circuit. "It was a lot of fun. We called it the barbecue circuit because every Friday after you qualified, they had a barbecue and the Calcutta," January said. "It was an opportunity because if you had a good guy buy you then you could get a caddy. And then if you played good and made him some money then maybe he would slip you a little."

Another major tournament winner, the 1971 Masters champion Charles Coody, played the West Texas circuit but once wandered over into East Texas to win a tournament:

In 1960 when I qualified for the U.S. Open as an amateur, I needed to come up with some money from somewhere to get to Denver. I won a tournament in Tyler and with the money I made selling the new set of irons and from the guy who bought me in the Calcutta, I was able to go.

Coody sees the demise of the barbecue circuit as depriving young golfers from a testing ground not available today:

When I was growing up in the 1950s, the local individual tournament was a means to measure yourself and see how good you were. The kids today are missing out because not everyone can afford to play in the junior tournaments and those are even a little selective as to who can play.

Andy Dillard grew up in Tyler and won the Texas state junior at age 15. He went on to play on a national championship college team at Oklahoma

State but says the barbecue tournaments were the best preparation for the pro tour. "I don't think the young players today realize how different it is to play for money than for a trophy. You learn to play golf under a different kind of pressure and that was what I loved about those tournaments."

Not only did a local high school golfer get the chance to play in a tournament with top amateurs, sometimes he was thrust into the company of the best players of that time. Benny Stubbs now works in the golf shop at Piney Woods Country Club in Nacogdoches, which has had an invitational for more than 60 years. Like most of the older tournaments, it has converted from individual play to a partnership. Stubbs played his golf growing up at Corsicana Country Club, an A.W. Tillinghast design. He is part of a large golfing family with his dad Gilbert having a fine amateur record in the late 1940s.

Stubbs said:

> I remember my dad taking me to Lampasas for a barbecue tournament when I was just a sophomore in high school. I qualified for the championship flight and drew Don January for my first match. I got 2-up on him through three holes and said to myself that I'm fixing to beat me a hotshot. Well, we walked in after 15 holes and I didn't win."

Howie Alexander of Tyler's Willow Brook Country Club had a similar experience in 1973:

> My dad had just bought me a new Mustang after I graduated from high school and Mark Triggs rode down to Center with me. We are still getting our clubs out of the trunk when someone hollers at us that we're on the tee. We run up to the first tee and we are paired with Crenshaw, Lietzke, and the reigning State Amateur champion Tony Pfaff. Mark may have been used to that company but I was just a high school kid who wanted to be good.

Jim Todd is a board member of the Texas Golf Association and a former equipment representative from Lufkin. He remembers his introduction to the beer and barbecue tour:

> I guess my most vivid impression was the first time I played in one of those tournaments. It was in Jacksonville and I was just a sophomore in high school. A couple of my older friends took me down with them and the first thing I know, I am on the practice tee next to Marty Fleckman and he is like a Greek god or something. There was no one in the world, in my mind then, who could hit the ball as well as he did. I couldn't imagine anything like that. And

going over to Center when I was in college, they had a better field than the NCAA.

Fleckman dominated the East Texas circuit for several years in the mid 1960s and led the U.S. Open through three rounds at Baltusrol in 1967 before giving way to a guy named Jack Nicklaus. He now teaches golf in Houston.

Even the great players were sometimes wowed by their colleagues. Billy Maxwell of Abilene won seven times on the PGA Tour and had an outstanding amateur career that included a U.S. Amateur title in 1951 at Saucon Valley in Bethlehem, Pennsylvania:

> *I tell you what I do remember about amateur golf back then. Nobody could touch Earl Stewart. We were all chasing him. There was a car dealer in Garland that bought Earl 30 times in the Calcutta and won 30 times. That's how good Earl Stewart was at that time. When Earl beat you, he just shook your hand and turned and went to the clubhouse. It didn't matter where you were, you were done. He wasn't rude but just a great competitor.*

Stewart later became the only club pro to win a PGA Tour event at his own course when he won the 1961 Dallas Open at Oak Cliff Country Club. His son Chip is currently a top senior amateur and also played the barbecue circuit in the 1960s.

Miller Barber grew up on the Texas side of Texarkana and was successful on both the PGA and Champions Tour, winning three U.S. Senior Opens in the span of four years during the mid 1980s. He laughed when asked his most vivid memory of the barbecue tournaments. "I remember one match in particular" the man they call *Mr. X* said:

> *It was at Kilgore and I played Dick Whetzel. He was one of those North Texas State golfers with Don January back then and he must have been 13 under because I was 12 under and he beat me one up. It was one of those matches where one of us birdied nearly every hole... But they called me up and said they wanted to dedicate a plaque to me. So I drove down and they said you used to drive it over this ditch and we want to name it after you. I said you've got to be kidding me. But really, it's quite an honor and I had a great time.*

The man responsible for honoring Barber is Terry Stembridge, a former sports announcer for the San Antonio Spurs who has moved back to his hometown of Kilgore and led an effort to rejuvenate the invitational tournament there:

We have had an individual champion here every year since 1937. In 2000 we decided to rename the tournament the Meadowbrook Classic and invited Miller down to dedicate the plaque in his honor. We had a fish fry and it was a lot of fun. Like most of the others, our tournament isn't what it once was but it is still a good tournament.

Barber described the East and West Texas barbecue circuits as little tours back when he was an amateur in the 1950s and that has now gone away.

Texas Golf Association director Rob Addington has a unique perspective on the changing of the amateur landscape in Texas. He played in some barbecue tournaments as a high school golfer and now is the top executive of the organization that regulates amateur golf in the state:

It (competition) has definitely changed, but whether it's for the better, I'm not sure. I played in my share of the tournaments during high school and college and there were a lot of characters and you learned how to play. You learned that not everyone has to have a great swing or the right equipment or dress right to be a good player. It was neat to see that and there were just some guys on certain courses that you could not beat. Some of that is lost.

I think junior golf has developed to such a point that we have a good junior tour. Both sections have their tournaments and there is a national organization so that some of the kids can play nationally. Some of it hasn't changed for the better. Did we all break the rules back then about the amateur status? Probably, but was anyone paying close attention? No, but now days people are paying closer attention to that, especially in Texas. It's a shame that it has died because of all of the golfing characters and the players that may not have played college golf but were still unbelievably good players. Guys that could get it up and down all day from the hard pan, with not the best equipment in the world, was something incredible to watch.

Addington is referring to an era when golf was fun and everybody in town turned up to watch the best players go at it for a trophy, a new set of irons, and maybe a shoebox full of cash to be handed over later in the parking lot.

Willow Brook Country Club

WELCOMES YOU TO ITS CHAMPIONSHIP

18 HOLE COURSE

It is my pleasure to invite you to join with us in this, our annual Invitational Golf Tournament. You will find our championship course in excellent condition and a full program of social activities has been planned for your further enjoyment. We hope you will be able to participate.

Sincerely

B. G. BYARS, President

Golf Tournament Winners

1948 EARL STEWART, Longview   1951 L. C. TAYLOR, Tyler

1949 RALEIGH SELBY, Kilgore   1952 BUSTER REED, Dallas

1950 RALEIGH SELBY, Kilgore   1953 COURSE UNDER REPAIR

1954 BENNY CASTLOO

OFFICIAL PROGRAM
AND
INVITATION

ANNUAL
AMATEUR INVITATIONAL

Golf Tournament

Willow Brook Country Club

TYLER, TEXAS

MAY

12 - 13 - 14 - 15

NINETEEN HUNDRED FIFTY-FIVE

Invitation to 1955 Willow Brook Invitational – please note entry fee
of $12.50 and 14 flights of 16 players each.
That's 224 men playing individual match play!

Mr. *Larry Barlow*

You are cordially invited to participate

in the *Annual Willow Brook Country Club*

Invitational Golf Tournament . . .

May 12 thru 15, 1955

INVITATION COMMITTEE
Gilbert Reeves
J. G. Walker, Jr.

INFORMATION

DATE—To be played May 13, 14, 15 over Willow Brook's 18 hole championship course.

QUALIFYING ROUNDS—Qualify with 18 holes any time between Thursday, May 5 and Thursday, May 12, 6 p.m. All trying for championship flight must declare themselves and be accompanied by official scorers. Medalist must qualify Thursday, May 12.

FLIGHTS—There will be a maximum of 14 flights. All flights will be composed of 16 players, except championship flight which will be composed of 32 players. The first match losers in championship flight will form the first flight. ALL MATCH PLAY. Use of carts prohibited in championship and first flights.

ENTRY FEE—$12.50 covers Tournament and all social activities for player and his wife.

$2,000.00 in Merchandise Prizes to be given to winners and runners up of all flights.

Invitation Committee
P. O. Box 157
Tyler, Texas

ENTERTAINMENT

THURSDAY NIGHT, May 12th
Calcutta Pool and Barbecue for men only
Welcoming Party

FRIDAY NIGHT, May 13th
Western Party with food served from Chuck Wagon, 6:30 to 9:30 P. M.
Fun & Frolic Style Show—Fashions modelled by Mayer & Schmidt models. Music by Western and Dance Band of Tyler Junior College Apaches.
Opening of Swimming Pool for players and their wives.

SATURDAY NIGHT, May 14th
Cocktail Party—6:00 P. M. to 8:00 P. M. for players and their wives.
Dinner Dance—9:00 P. M. to 1:00 A. M. featuring Jimmy Joy's Troubadours.

SUNDAY, May 15th
Finals in all Flights—Swimming—Awards to Winners—Buffet Dinner

NOTE: Entry Fee Does Not Include Food Other Than Calcutta Pool Barbecue.
Buffet Luncheon will be served each day in Men's Grill Room for convenience of contestants.

The Calcutta

"All right folks, you know that Jimmy's a heck of player so can I get two hundred? Got two hundred, give me three."

The Auctioneer

Somewhere in East Texas

The origins of the Calcutta betting pools go back to the Royal Calcutta Turf Club founded in the East Indian city in 1820. The turf club is still operating but since 2001 the city changed its official name from Calcutta to Kolkata.

Horse racing actually began in India before the founding of the turf club and pari-mutuel betting was introduced in 1792. That form of betting is where money is wagered according to the previous performance of the competitors. The monies wagered are pooled and then awarded according to the results of the race. This type of betting became known as a Calcutta pool when applied to golf and other competitions.

Along with horse races there were also polo matches at the turf club. It seems horses and golf have been linked in the United States since both sports made their way across the Atlantic Ocean.

In Aiken, South Carolina, The Palmetto Club is one of the oldest courses in the United States, founded in 1892. This exclusive club once spurned a request to play from the President, William Howard Taft, because he would not be accompanied by a member. Across the street from the club and equally old in years is a polo field and racetrack. Every March there is a three-year-old thoroughbred review held there prior to racing season with men and women dressed in Southern finery.

"It is Mint Juleps in sterling silver goblets or beer straight from the can," Darlene Walters of South Carolina said. "Everyone enjoys the Aiken

Steeplechase. Flowers are set at each tent, an array of food, women wearing hats akin to the Kentucky Derby, and the horse racing is great, too."

Another example of horse racing and golf co-existing is at The Country Club in Brookline, Massachusetts, where amateur Francis Quimet put American golf on the map in 1913 by defeating British professionals Harry Vardon and Ted Ray. It is the subject of the one of the best movies about golf, *The Greatest Game Ever Played*.

The oldest golf resort in America is at Pinehurst, North Carolina where a visitor will find an old racetrack just across the way from the famous Number Two course that has hosted a couple of U.S. Opens in the past 15 years, including the memorable 1999 championship won on the last hole by the late Payne Stewart.

At the old beer and barbecue tournaments, the Calcutta was typically held the night before the first round and the players were auctioned off to create the total pool of money bet. A rider was sometimes used and it involved a small amount of money placed for a blind draw of the players. That small amount would entitle its owner to a small percentage of a player's winnings. The rider helped prime the pump, so to speak, before the auctioning of the players.

Once the tournament was over, the pool was split, typically 40 percent to the winner; 20 percent to second; 10 percent to third and fourth; and 5 percent to fifth, sixth, seventh and eighth place. Ties resulted in those percentages being shared.

Gambling of some sort has been a part of golf since its inception. Competitive golf can be a game of intense bravado or ego, if you will. The governing bodies of the game, the Royal and Ancient Golfing Society of Great Britain and the United States Golf Association address gambling in their rule books.

According to the USGA, gambling is permitted if it is in the spirit of friendly competition and not solely for financial gain. Calcutta betting is especially frowned upon and participation in such an endeavor "may endanger his Amateur Status."

That admonishment never deterred those who loved quality amateur golf from having a good time at the beer and barbecue tournaments. A Longview newspaper of 1948 even cited the dignitaries present at the Premier Oil Company's sixth annual barbecue party attended by more than 1,200 guests. The dignitaries included United States senatorial candidate Lyndon Baines Johnson, who would later become the thirty-sixth President of the United States. A photo of the Calcutta board does not show LBJ buying anyone that night.

SECTION I: EAST TEXAS

West Virginia is the strangest place I've even seen... except for East Texas.."

M.B. Woofter (Paw Paw)

Kilgore, Texas

The Blond Bomber Returns

"He had those Popeye forearms and could really hit it."

John Pigg

Austin, Texas

The summer sounds of crickets and frogs filled the air as a heavy dusk fell in deep East Texas. A row of cars surrounded the green to provide needed light as day turned to night at Center Country Club.

Looking over a right to left breaking putt of some 10 feet on this lovely evening in 1973 was the already famous Ben Crenshaw of Austin. With stylishly long blond hair and a confidence that was unmistakable even to the casual observer, Crenshaw took his time to see the proper line on a Bermuda green that this late in the day was "as grainy as barbed wire."

Before there was Tiger Woods there was Ben Crenshaw. Both were child prodigies in golf.

Woods did the unthinkable as an amateur winning three consecutive USGA junior titles before adding three straight USGA amateurs. But before the world had ever heard of Tiger Woods, a natural athlete from Austin with a stocky build and blond hair dominated junior golf in Texas in the late 1960s. On a smaller stage, he had every bit the aura of Arnold Palmer.

Crenshaw won the state junior at Brackenridge Park in San Antonio as a fifteen-year-old in 1967 and again in 1969, shooting under par for the 72-hole competition. In 1968, he won the state Jaycees tournament in Abilene, which qualified him for the national competition in Tulsa that he also won. His legend in junior golf culminated two years later when he rolled his tee shot across a bridge on the final hole to maintain a one-shot lead and win the Texas Oklahoma Junior in Wichita Falls. That bridge was named in his honor but has since been removed with a recent renovation to the Weeks Park Golf Course.

Though he never won a U.S. Amateur, Crenshaw won three NCAA individual championships in his three years of college golf and nine other national tournaments such as the Southern, Eastern, Western, Northeast, and Susquehanna amateurs. The icing on the cake was being low amateur at the Masters. So when *The Blond Bomber* came to Center in 1972, it is doubtful that anyone with more pedigree ever teed it up in a beer and barbecue tournament in East Texas.

And just what was the attraction of this tournament played on a nine-hole course in a tiny town of about 5,000 people near the Louisiana border? Was it the large Calcutta that might mean some serious spending money for college golfers? Certainly that was part of it, but the pull to play was much more than that. It was a chance to compete against the best of his peers and to do so in an atmosphere of small-town America. A family would put you up for the week and local galleries would number in the hundreds.

Billy Bob Thomason is a native of Center and was active in the tournament for many years. He lost in the finals of the first tournament in 1958. That was the only year that match play decided the champion. In the subsequent years, Thomason was more involved in recruiting players for the impressive field:

> We used to send out letters to get the players to come here but after a while we didn't have to do that. Players started contacting us to find out when the tournament was and how to get entered. The coaches liked to send their players here. Dave Williams (former longtime University of Houston coach) *even came up once. He called one time and asked for a favor and we said we would do anything for him because of all the help he had been through the years. He said he wanted us to let a little tow-headed high school boy from Bellaire play in our tournament. We said sure and that was the first of five straight years that Tom Jenkins played here. He never won but a lot of other good players never won here.*

Like a lot of the people in Center and surrounding towns such as Garrison and Timpson, Charles Rushing worked in the poultry business for many years and his family was involved in the tournament each summer. "It was such an occurrence to have all of the top college players come to your little hometown," Rushing said. "I remember watching Crenshaw hit out of a sand trap and he seemed mad with the result. I just thought even the great ones don't always do it just right."

Rushing continued:

> My son and the local kids would caddy and we had Willie Wood stay with us a couple of years and Mark Brooks one year. We got involved in the Calcutta. Me and about ten or fifteen guys would put in $300 or so each and then meet and try to decide who to buy.

We never did too much good but my wife and her little syndicate of ten or so women won one year. That's what made it so much fun.

The fun stretched all week during the tournament. "Friday night was a cocktail party for the players in the backyard of a prominent citizen's home and then there was a dance at the club on Saturday night featuring a big-name band," Rushing said. "The players were like family and come Sunday afternoon, there would be crowds of around five hundred or so at the club."

In 1972 Crenshaw was the highest seller in the Calcutta but failed to win. Bruce Lietzke defeated University of Houston teammate Arthur Russell in a playoff that year "in the dead of night," according to another University of Houston golfer, Bill Rogers.

Crenshaw thus had some unfinished business in 1973 when he returned to Center. It was his last tournament as an amateur and he wanted to go out a winner. He also wanted to win like former University of Texas teammates Dean Overturf (1971) and George Machock (1970).

The stage was set for Crenshaw that summer. As usual, the Calcutta was a spectacle under the pine trees adorned with Christmas lights. Everyone was suitably lubricated with beer and barbecued chicken when the flatbed truck rolled out and the auctioneer began to sell the players. It was nothing for someone to get a little too much beer and do something silly like flick on the siren of the sheriff's car. In rural Shelby County, he never bothered to lock the doors. Once again, Crenshaw sold for a bundle and that meant he had to win the tournament for his buyer to make a profit.

A harbinger of good things for Crenshaw occurred during the long drive contest Thursday afternoon. The players all would ante up $20 and get three balls to hit. He won the contest and stuffed plenty of cash into his pockets. "People don't realize, because of his condition now, just how long he was in college. He had those Popeye forearms and could really hit it," said John Pigg of Austin and a native of Center. "You could have put a towel over all three of his drives."

Rogers, a Texarkana native who would go on to play the tour and win the 1981 British Open, said a lot of his peers were in awe of Crenshaw during his college days:

I'm telling you that he was special. He had a great pro career but as an amateur he was a combination of Seve Ballesteros and I don't know who. He had his own personality with a bit of a temper that he used to make him play better... One time at the Border Olympics (72-hole college tournament in Laredo), he made a nine on the first hole and then went on to the win the tournament by ten shots. And the field wasn't a slouch, we were there and so were a lot of other good teams.

Crenshaw's thin physique now doesn't resemble the heft of his younger years. He also had a tremendous shoulder turn and moved his head from side to side a bit to generate his power. His putting stroke was long and silky and he had that knack for making the crucial putt when he needed it.

The field at Center that year was as strong as ever but it all came down to a ten-foot birdie putt for Crenshaw on the final hole of the tournament. In typical beer and barbecue fashion, car lights surrounded the ninth green down near a pond on the Center Country Club course. As legions of spectators, many with a cold beer in hand, looked on, Crenshaw used his much admired flowing putting stroke to glide the ball atop the "grainy as barbed wire" Bermuda grass and into the cup. His victory came at the expense of Pigg, a fine player at nearby Stephen F. Austin University, who was trying to win for the hometown gallery.

Pigg said:

Ben stayed with our family both times he came to Center. He was not a happy camper when he didn't do well the first year. He may have been too concerned about where he was going fishing that first year but he came back and won it. And me three-putting that final green helped him out.

Crenshaw turned pro soon afterwards and like another legend of the East Texas beer and barbecue circuit, Marty Fleckman of Port Arthur, won his debut tournament on the PGA Tour. He would go on to win 19 times with two of those at the Masters and was the winning captain of the memorable 1999 Ryder Cup.

In the Dead of Night

That was when I found out that they don't have co-champions in Center, Texas.

Bruce Lietzke

Athens, Texas

Bill Rogers still has an East Texas accent as thick as a milkshake at Guy's Orange Stand in his hometown of Texarkana, Texas. So when he exclaimed that his most vivid memory of the beer and barbecue days was when his University of Houston teammate and close friend to this day, Bruce Lietzke, defeated another University of Houston teammate Art Russell in the "dead of night," some might think his account a slight embellishment of the facts.

Not so says the tall and friendly protagonist of this tale, known to his friends as Leaky. Lietzke said:

> *I remember that tournament. It was getting so dark that with two holes to play, I considered quitting. But people said no, you have to finish. When we finished putting on the last hole, it was really dark, crazy dark. So we go into the pro shop and they take about 30 minutes to add up all of the scores and so forth. By now, it is about 10 at night in the middle of the summer. The guy gets up says, "boys, we have a tie between Bruce Lietzke and Arthur Russell."*

At that, Lietzke said he went over to Russell and congratulated him as a co-champion.

"That is pretty cool," Lietzke remembers saying:

Then whoever had me whispered into my ear that we don't have co-champions in Center. So I asked them if we were coming back the next morning or doing a scorecard playoff and they said no... It was obvious that they had done this before because soon there were about ten or fifteen cars that drove out of the parking lot and onto a fairway going away from the clubhouse. There were five or six cars on each side of the fairway with their headlights on, shining into the fairway. And a guy had a flashlight to help you tee up the ball and see the ball when you swung.

So we had this playoff at 10:15 or 10:30 at night. I can just remember thinking that you have to hit it inside the headlights so that you can find the ball. I hit a good one but Arthur hit one into the blackness of night and we never found his ball. I finished the hole and Arthur had to hit another ball and that was it. That was when I found out that they don't have co-champions in Center, Texas.

Rogers remembers the nine-hole track that the players just kept going around as they played 36 holes on the final day. A good test of golf built by the members with the help of longtime Tyler pro Ralph Morgan, the Center course had a good variety of holes but four trips around it in one day could do tricks to the mind.

Lietzke would go on to win thirteen times on the PGA Tour and seven times on the Champions Tour. One bit of trivia about Lietzke is that he is the only man to win the Byron Nelson Classic and Colonial twice. His first win at the Nelson at Preston Trail in 1981 was the last time an over par score for 72 holes was good enough to win a regular tour event.

Rogers won the 1981 British Open during a five-year run of good play from 1978 until 1983. Known as the *Panther* because of his gait while surveying a green for a chip or long putt, Rogers said he and Lietzke were present during a most interesting evening following the 1980 British Open at Muirfield, Scotland. Rogers explained:

It was a few hours after Watson had won the Open and we were all in the dining room having dinner. Whenever Ben (Crenshaw) would go over there, people would inundate him with gifts like books and they had given him some feathery balls and wooden shafted clubs. We were all toasting Tom and in a celebratory mood and somebody said, "Lets go play 10 and 18!"

It was mostly Americans, you know, the ugly Americans, and we jump up and go out. We blew up the feathery balls but kept playing and sure enough, the captain of the club, his name was Hamner or something, and man he was not enamored at all. He was upset and felt like it was a disgrace for us to do that. He came charging out on the 18th green and wanted to know what we are doing and Watson had just won the Open a couple of hours before. And now he is giving us the riot act. I ran into a pot bunker and tried to hide. I was that scared.

An account of the episode is now part of the lore of the Open Championship and proudly displayed in the halls outside of the bar at the Grey Walls Hotel adjacent to the splendid course.

Rogers, like Lietzke, a humble and extremely likeable man, seems almost embarrassed to discuss his 1981 British Open triumph. He prevailed over a young Bernhard Langer and bounced back from a double bogey early in the round to claim the *Claret Jug*. That trophy was displayed for a year proudly in an East Texas bank in Texarkana.

Rogers described:

A local bank asked if they could house if for the year and they built a case for it. There were a lot of people in the four states area (Texas, Arkansas, Oklahoma, and Louisiana) that came to see it after the word spread. There were stories of people coming a long way to see it. Going home with it was fun because the pilot acknowledged it and I even passed it around the plane. It was fun looking at all the names on it. Every square inch is filled with a name.

Rogers is also sometimes kidded about his austere ways with money and he recounted one of his first trips to a barbecue tournament, the Briarwood Invitational in Tyler:

I had a crisp $100 bill that Jerry Robinson (his home course golf pro) gave me when I left for Tyler and I was consumed with the thought of that money the whole way down. I pulled into a barbecue place and ordered something and then pulled out than $100 bill and some young girl said they couldn't make change for it. I had a lot of pride about carrying that money down to the tournament.

Robinson said a few years later that Rogers came home with about $95.

Lietzke and Rogers enjoyed their days on the barbecue circuit just like they enjoy their friendship today. They were Crenshaw's assistant captains at the 1999 Ryder Cup when the Americans came storming back to win at The Country Club. It has been a sweet ride for the two guys.

The Scots may have given us the game but unlike the folks at Muirfield, East Texas golfers like to have some fun. Lietzke can attest to that after his real life *Tin Cup* experience in the dead of night in Deep East Texas. "That's just East Texas," Lietzke said. "They had their way of doing things and it was a tradition. It was great to see that my friends like Don January and Miller Barber and others like Billy Martindale and Billy Maxwell, all played those tournaments. It left a lasting impression on me. During the summertime, we would travel up and down East Texas having fun and playing golf."

Dick Martin of Dallas, center, is flanked on the left by Ben Hogan and on the right by Henry Ransom circa the late 1940s

The Little Man Who Could Play

"I always asked Dick why he didn't turn pro and he said he couldn't afford to."

Billy Bob Thomason

Center, Texas

When they buried Dick Martin in 1989, less than a mile from his beloved home course Tenison Park, they laid his trusty 9-iron across his chest. Martin could work magic with that 9-iron. He used it to make a pot full of money through the years at Tenison and just about every other course throughout Texas and into Arkansas and Oklahoma.

Long time Dallas pro Eldridge Miles said:

I played him one time at the old Texas Women's University course in Denton and the greens were as hard as concrete. He beat me one up because my ball would bounce and roll over the green but his would take a hop or two and then stop on a dime. Later I looked in his bag and it was a ladies 9-iron but the grooves were so deep and wide that you would cut your thumb if you rubbed it over the face... But you couldn't help but love the little guy, even when he was taking your money, because he had that twinkle in his eye. And boy could he play.

Martin's standard bet at Tenison in his prime, according to Tyler's A.J. Triggs, was that he could take the 9-iron, a 5-iron, and putter and shoot 33 or better on the front nine. "And you didn't want to take that bet," Triggs said. "He would beat you eight out of 10 times."

Like a lot of other golfers from Dallas such as Bob Rawlins, Triggs learned to play golf in the late 1940s at *T Park*, not far from the Cotton

Bowl, and soon came to know Martin. Martin was pint sized, probably only 5 foot 6 at the most. He wore his cap tilted to one side and always said that he wanted to play for something, a bowl of ice cream, he would say with a little wink.

A terrific player, Martin won just about every tournament on the barbecue circuit, most notably the Premier Invitational in Longview during the 1950s and the Center Invitational in 1963. At Center he preceded winners with more famous golfing names such as Homero Blancas and Marty Fleckman. As was recently mentioned on television, he has the amateur record for most under par at the Byron Nelson when it was the Dallas Open in 1957 and played at the now defunct Glen Lakes Country Club.

Martin was a guy who played every day of the year at Tenison or in an amateur tournament somewhere during the summer. Though small, he could move the golf ball and his short game was impeccable during his best years. "Dick could do whatever he wanted to do with the golf ball," longtime friend Jerry Biesel, a Dallas attorney, recalled. "Once he intentionally hit a five iron over a green with a lake in front of it and as experienced a guy as A.J. Triggs was fooled into hitting it into the water. Of course Dick got up and down because that was never a problem."

Triggs does not dispute that story but said the irony of it is that Martin saw his best chance of winning the Briarwood Invitational in Tyler disappear in the early 1960s when he hit his ball into the edge of the water on the same hole. He attempted to splash it out onto the green and proceeded to make a seven to eliminate himself from contention.

His crowd from Tenison Park was an assortment of gamblers who could play some golf. Those in his entourage would often arrive at the barbecue tournament en masse. There was Biesel who was known as the *Little Lawyer*, Railroad Red Whitehead, and the Beasley brothers, Charles and Leroy, just to name a few. Biesel said:

> We had so much fun on those trips. Ole Red was a golf nut and would have all of his clubs out in the hotel room and talk to them before his round. He would say to one wedge, "you are coming with me today so act right." It was hilarious and after our rounds we would all go to dinner or get ice cream. We just all got along and those were some great days.

Lee Trevino was known to play in some of the money games at Tenison Park. "Trevino said that Dick was the best player he knew until he met Jack Nicklaus," Biesel said from his Dallas office. "I went all over the state with him and out to Vegas for some money games. He was 76 when he passed away. I loved the guy and still miss him."

One time Dick was in my office and Trevino called. He said they were rained out the first day at the Texas Open in San Antonio and for me to get Dick and come on down. We get down there and we are following Trevino the next day and there was a huge crowd. This was in Lee's heyday and you can imagine the Hispanic following he had then. He has this pitch and run shot from about 75 yards onto an undulating green. He darn near holes it and the crowd goes nuts and then he quiets them down and calls Dick out of the gallery into the fairway and announces to everyone that "this is the man who taught me that shot" and they hugged. It was a great moment.

Like so many other veteran players, Triggs remembers Martin from his best years at Tenison Park. "Let me tell you something. In his day he was something else," Triggs said. "He would make plenty of money on the putting green from about 10 am until noon and then hit the course. I have seen him go around that putting green and ace every hole. And you can ask Trevino or Don January and they will tell you just how good he was."

Martin and his group were robbed once while playing in Dallas and it must have been an inside job since one of the armed banditos told one of the golfers by name not to move. Their identity was concealed by the hosiery over their faces, but Biesel said the crime was later solved and most of the stolen money returned. The newspapers reported $1,500 stolen but Martin later told a friend that it was about ten times that much. He didn't want anyone to know just how much money he and his buddies were carrying around during those days.

A photograph of Martin from his early days on the barbecue circuit appeared in the *Longview Journal* and he was described as the "dapper amateur from Dallas." Martin was also a businessman who never passed up a chance to make money. "He would pick up bottles and later turn them in for some money," Triggs said. "He never passed up a chance to make a dime."

No one can recall if Martin ever had a job but he always had plenty of money. And if you looked in the trunk of his Cadillac, you would think it was a pro shop. "I used to ask Dick why he didn't turn pro," Billy Bob Thomason of Center said. "He would always tell me that he couldn't afford to. He was making more money hustling than he could have made on tour in those days."

Martin also was coy about his age. "I asked him one time how old he was," Thomason said. "And he said 'I've been 55 for quite a few years now.'"

A good gambler knows when to hold 'em and when to fold 'em. Martin was a good gambler. Sale Omohundro, the owner and pro at Woodlawn Country Club in Sherman said:

> *My dad* (Read) *told me that he and Miller Barber went down to Tenison to play Dick Martin and Art Corbin. Now this was before anyone knew Miller and he makes six birdies and two bogeys the first nine and my dad pars the two holes Miller bogeyed. They are up about a grand at the turn and Corbin says they will double the bets on the back. Dick pulls out his money and said "no, it's time for these boys to head on back to Sherman."*

Omohundro also recalls that at the tender age of 12 he was allowed to go and caddy for Martin on one his runs through Oklahoma. His dad told Martin that his son could go as long as he wouldn't try to beat him out of his money shooting dice before they got back to Sherman. "He asked me straight up before we were out of the parking lot if I wanted a flat rate or a percentage," Omohundro said. "I was only 12 but I knew to take the percentage deal. I think he liked that."

Just how good was Dick Martin? Ever the *Little Lawyer*, Biesel offers two final arguments. The first case study was Martin's low amateur showing at the 1957 Dallas Open at Glen Lakes Country Club. He shot a 72-hole total of five under par but Biesel contends that Martin was not showing all of his skills. "Dick told me that he had a hard enough time getting a game back then and didn't want to go too low."

The second story took place in Houston at about the same time. "We were down at Champions Club in Houston one time and Jackie Burke was kidding Dick about some tournament they played in years before. He said 'Dick, why didn't you let me win that luggage that time because you knew how much I liked it and how much I wanted it?'

"Well, Dick told him, 'I ran into a guy in the pro shop before the tournament and sold him that luggage. Of course, I had to win it before I could deliver it.'"

Case closed. A patriarch of the barbecue circuit, Dick Martin of Tenison Park was just that good.

Premier

"It was a course that weaved through the refinery."

Roy Pace

Longview, Texas

Don Cherry said that Texas is really two states; East Texas and West Texas. For many years there were two distinct barbecue tours that ran concurrently so that a good player seldom ventured from his part of the state. The courses were disparate, too. Unlike the flat and barren courses of West Texas, those in East Texas featured hilly terrain with plenty of trees that were infested with creeks and lakes.

An abandoned Premier service station on U.S. Highway 80 outside of Gladewater, Texas

A lot of the nine-hole courses played on the East Texas circuit were built in the 1920s and 1930s and designed by local golfers or Texas golf pioneers such as John Bredemus. Much has been written about the eccentric bon vivant who was praised by Harvey Penick for his love of the game. He had an aversion to playing with new golf balls and subsisted on a diet of snacks during his later years. In East Texas, Bredemus is credited with designing Henderson Country Club and may have influenced several more.

No one is sure who designed the nine-hole course at the Premier Refinery outside of Longview in a community once known as Greggton. But it was unique and downright weird. It featured holes that were routed around oil tanks and a par three at the bottom of the course where players sometimes used putters since a wedge off of hardpan had to be punched low under a canopy of trees. The green was bordered by a pond on the left and since the slope was deemed slightly unfair, boards were used to prevent the ball from running into the water, ala miniature golf. Today, the property is padlocked and remains untouched since being closed in the late 1970s.

Growing up just down the road from Premier, one of eight brothers and two sisters, was Jacky Cupit. While he won three times on tour and almost won the 1963 U.S. Open, some locals would say he was not the best of his clan. That distinction, they would say, belonged to his older brother Buster who didn't like the travel and stayed off the tour in favor of running his own course, the Longview Country Club. Another brother, Bobby, won a few of the East Texas tournaments.

The record, however, points to Jacky.

"For a few years in the early 1960s, nobody could beat Jacky," Terry Stembridge of Kilgore said. "He was practically unbeatable and if he didn't win, it was an upset."

The Premier tournament was played on its quirky course for many years. In the heart of the East Texas Oil field, the tournament started in 1942. According to Rick Maxey, a Longview native who won his share of barbecue tournaments during the 1970s and grew up caddying for his

Earl Stewart, Jr. putts at the Premier golf course as
Wilford Wehrle and his caddy watch during the finals of the 1946 tournament

father, Preacher Maxey, at Premier in the early 1960s, the first tournament replaced an annual skeet shoot put on by the owner of Premier Refinery, the flamboyant Sylvester Dayson.

"They couldn't get enough ammunition for the skeet shoot in 1942 and Mr. Dayson said, 'well, let's have a golf tournament or something,'" Maxey said. "Needless to say, it really caught on and there were some great tournaments through the years."

Gaining momentum during the late 1940s just after America had prevailed in World War II, the Calcutta barbecue, according to the *Longview Journal*, drew crowds as large as twelve hundred people.

"That was the biggest tournament of the year," Roy Pace of Longview said. "It was played on that little golf course but it got the strongest field and had the biggest Calcutta. It was really something."

Pace is a former touring and teaching pro who moved back to Longview from Connecticut in 2000. He now runs the Alpine Target Golf Center that is the *Home of the Divine Nine*, a lighted par three course. He won the Premier in 1961 and was defending champion when Homero Blancas shot his 55 to win the 1962 tournament.

Roy Pace continued:

It was so competitive. A lot of good players and I remember the year I won was in a playoff against Fred Marti. The year that Homero shot the 55, I was the defending champion and after 54 holes, we were tied at 9 under. I shoot 67 and lose by 12 strokes. He (Marti) was leading. He had a four-shot lead at 13 under and shoots 66. He then calls home and his father asked him what he shot and he said 66. So his dad said what did you win by? And Fred said to his dad, "I lost by seven."

The driving force behind the Premier tournament for years was Dayson, who was partners with J.R. Parten, a successful oilman who was influential in Texas politics. Parten headed up a commission appointed by the federal government to oversee construction of the *Big Inch Pipeline* from Longview to New Jersey. The pipeline was built within a year in 1942 to facilitate the energy needs of the Allied forces in Europe and thus contributed to the victory.

Dayson and Parten were players both economically and politically during the immediate years after World War II. There are pictures from the 1948 Premier tournament that show Lyndon Johnson attending the Calcutta barbecue as part of his successful campaign for a US Senate seat that year. There were also a bevy of influential oil men who were flown in for the tournament.

Eventually Dayson and Parten sold the refinery and the tournament began to wane. It was supplanted by the American Classic that was held at Pinecrest Country Club, a short but challenging course across town from Premier that was always in good shape. The Pinecrest tournament drew good fields throughout the 1970s.

One of the winners of the American Classic tournament during the early 1970s was Stan Altgelt of Corpus Christi. Altgelt, who passed away in 2006, shot a second-round 63 en route to his win and though never a star on the PGA Tour, he did lead it in driving distance in 1973 with what seems a paltry average drive of 279 yards. This was the era of persimmon before metal woods and the golf balls were made of soft balata rubber.

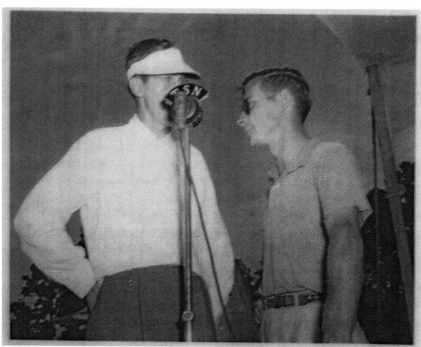

Earl Stewart, Jr., right, is interviewed after his win at Premier in 1946.
Please note Stewart's powerful left forearm

55

"It has been embellished a lot through the years but one thing is true, Homero shot 55 and I got beat."

Fred Marti

Baytown, Texas

T.C. Hamilton is one of those guys who is about seventy and still looks like he is forty. He is trim with plenty of hair and very little of it gray. The former greens superintendent at Dallas Country Club, Hamilton was quite a player in his younger days and still gets it around the course pretty well. He led his Tyler Lee high school team to a Texas state championship in 1959 and won the Briarwood Invitational that summer, beating the seemingly unbeatable Jacky Cupit among others in an impressive field.

But at the 1962 Premier Invitational, Hamilton missed the cut and did not qualify to play 36 holes on Sunday with a chance to win the championship. So Hamilton picked up his friend that everyone called *Toad*, iced down a case of beer and headed from Tyler to Longview in his Ford Falcon. He wanted to watch his good friend Fred Marti, who was leading the tournament.

Marti, the son of the golf pro at the Humble Oil Company (Exxon) course on the gulf coast at Baytown, was playing some great golf. He fired rounds of 66-66 for a 132 on Saturday to lead defending champion Roy Pace of Longview by several shots while his University of Houston teammate Homero Blancas was further back at 139.

Hamilton remembers arriving at the course while the players were having lunch. He learned that Marti had shot a 64 in the morning but lost two shots to Blancas who had a 62. Now tied with Blancas was Pace and both were still five shots behind.

"You just liked being around Fred Marti," Hamilton said. "He was so relaxed, so laid back and fun to watch. Homero was the same way. I guess you can be relaxed when you played as well as they did back then."

Hamilton remembers watching the final round with the cooler of beer safely stashed at a central location near the office of the Premier Refinery. The little nine-hole course weaved through the refinery and the corporate offices were conveniently near the middle of the golf course. That way Hamilton and Toad could pass the cooler every two or three holes and not get too dehydrated on a hot August day in East Texas.

"It's funny but I remember Blancas missing a couple of very makeable putts though he made some long ones coming in," Hamilton said. "On the second or third hole, a dogleg par-five, he nearly hit the green and then chipped up to about four feet and missed it."

In the *Legends of Texas Golf*, Blancas remembers a young kid skidding to a stop on his bike nearby just as he was hitting his putt. The loud shrieking noise caused Blancas to jam the putt. Obviously things were a little looser around the course in 1962.

The nonchalance factor was even more evident at the final hole when Hamilton said he had to ask Marti to drive the Falcon down the fairway so they could watch the finish. Marti gladly obliged, knowing no doubt that in spite of shooting another 66, he was just playing for second place with Blancas needing a birdie on the par-five to shoot the lyrical 55.

Blancas made it interesting. With a throng that had swelled to about one hundred or more people, Blancas proceeded to shove his drive straight towards the road and out of bounds. The ball slammed against a tree and rebounded into the fairway, but a long distance from the green. So Blancas laid the ball up with a 4-iron and then wedged to about four feet. The son of the greens keeper from Houston was deadly with his wedge game.

"I told myself to just ram it into the back of the cup," Blancas said. "I had 24-year-old nerves but I just froze over the ball and finally hit a putt that just barely got over the front edge of the cup."

The gallery loved it but it took a while for the number to sink in. Blancas had just shot a 55, 15 under par for one round. He said he really had lost count of where he stood with par until a person informed him on the final tee that a birdie four would give him the 55.

Hamilton said:

I do think most people were a little stunned by the score. The thing that hit me was that he had played 36 holes at 23 under. That is just amazing and takes a while to sink in, and he missed a couple of putts that he could have made. But that last one I remember being longer than four feet and he made a really long one on the next to the last hole. So it wasn't like he didn't make some putts. Of course you can't shoot 55 without making some putts.

Some want to lessen the achievement by saying it was on an easy course but Marti wants no part of that:

They had some strange holes and it wasn't a long course but I wouldn't say it was that easy, not with all of the out of bounds on it. A guy named Jim Fetters was leading the first day when he tried to hit a high ball on one par-four where you could bounce the ball off of an oil tank and on to the green. He kept hitting balls into the tank that bounced the wrong way and were out of bounds on the refinery property. After four balls out of bounds, he walked in.

They even had one hole that was a 180-yard par-four but not easy. It was a ninety-degree dogleg so you had to hit about a 6-iron and then a wedge. They had a circle drawn around the green about twenty feet out that was out of bounds if you went over the corner to try to hit the green with your drive. Needless to say, they had a lot of local rules.

About his famous phone call to his dad after the tournament when he mentioned that he had a seven-shot lead and shot 66 to lose by four, Marti said, "It has been embellished a lot through the years but one thing is true, Homero shot a 55 and I got beat."

Marti was indeed a fine player on both the barbecue circuit and later on the PGA Tour. He never won a tour event but made a good living for several years before returning to the gulf coast to teach golf in Baytown.

Blancas now lives in Houston near the Champions Golf Club and advocates an emphasis on the short game for players coming up today. As the son of the greens superintendent of River Oaks Country Club, Blancas would chip and putt for hours when he was a boy. He would often play at night and was always a master with a wedge. And he still enjoys being known as *Mr. 55*.

Speaking with a reporter some twenty years ago during a break at a Champions Tour event in Pensacola, Florida, Blancas was asked what was more meaningful to him, winning a tour event such as the Colonial in 1970 or the 55 at the little course outside of Longview.

"I have to say the 55," Blancas said. "That was special and it became my calling card. I was known for being able to go low. I have had people ask me what my choking point was and I always say that it must be 15 under because I got to 14 under and birdied the next hole."

Hamilton was one of those lucky enough to see it.

Homero Blancas, Mr. 55, during his college days at the University of Houston

The Briar Patch

"I always thought Briarwood was the Masters..."

Guy Cullins

Kerrville, Texas

The Briarwood Invitational in Tyler was another prominent tournament started in 1958 and always played the first weekend in August. Originally a nine-hole course near Lake Bellwood on the west side of Tyler, Briarwood converted to 18 holes in the early 1960s and was considered one of the best courses played on the barbecue circuit of East Texas. It was hilly with natural sandy roughs that played havoc on errant drives and had tiny "pushed up" greens with plenty of break. For those reasons, Tyler's A.J. Triggs, was perennially the man to beat. He was short and straight off the tee but deadly with his wedge and putter.

Triggs won the inaugural tournament in 1958 and again in 1965 and lost a playoff to David Price of Odessa in 1972 for a third title. Price, director of golf at Bent Tree Golf Club in Dallas, remembers the tournament well. Price described it:

I had just graduated from college... We both parred the first hole and on the second hole, A.J. pitched up to about two or three feet and everyone from Tyler was saying "give it to him, give it to him, give it to him" and I had a fifteen foot birdie putt so I gave it to him and then I hit it two or three feet past and nobody said anything!

So then I had to tap in my putt and we went to the next hole which was not a real long par-five and I hit a really good tee shot and he hit it into the right rough in an almost unplayable position so that it took him a couple of shots to get back on the fairway. I had

*something like a six-iron to the green. I hit it on the green and had
an eagle putt from 40 and knocked it up for an easy two putt and
I'm not even sure if he finished the hole. But he has been such a
wonderful guy and has been a good friend for almost 40 years.*

A highly respected rules expert with the PGA of America, Price also
smiles at another detail of the playoff. "I've often thought about it," Price
said. "The tournament was stroke play so the playoff should have been as
well but it was played as match play."

As for Triggs, he had his share of wins and laughs at the Briarwood
tournament, one he played in for more than 20 consecutive years:

*I played in 21 straight and thought it emerged as a top college field
in those days. One year (1960) the Calcutta was $38 thousand at
Briarwood and me and (Jacky) Cupit and (Billy) Martindale sold
for $19 thousand of it.*

Triggs has many stories but one he finds particularly funny and
indicative of his role through the years at Briarwood:

*The Oklahoma State boys sat in front of me on the bleachers at
Briarwood one year and one of them asked who was leading.
"Some old fart who can't hit it anywhere shot a 66," one of them
said. I leaned over and tapped one of them on the shoulder and
said, "Let me introduce myself, I'm Old Fart."*

Cupit and Martindale were forces in East Texas in the late 1950s and
early 1960s. Cupit won the 1960 Briarwood tournament and did not make
a score higher than a four for 54 holes. That year the Briarwood course was
still nine holes but not easy.

Briarwood and Tyler proved to be fertile ground for Fleckman, another
in a long line of University of Houston standouts. He won the Briarwood
Invitational in 1963 and 1964 and also won the Texas State Amateur across
town at Willow Brook Country Club in 1964. Before turning pro and
winning his first event, the Cajun Classic, Fleckman was leading the 1967
U.S. Open through three rounds at storied Baltusrol. He stumbled to an 80
on Sunday as Jack Nicklaus won his second of four U.S. Opens.

It wasn't long before another Triggs appeared on the scene at
Briarwood Country Club. A.J.'s oldest son Mark was shooting par golf by
the time he was thirteen years old at Willow Brook across town. He first
won the Briarwood Invitational after his senior year in high school in 1971.
He won again in 1973.

The younger Triggs said:

What I remember most was a shot that I hit on the 17th hole the first time that I won. I remember your dad (Crutcher Wheeler) was watching me and there was a gap in the row of pines on that hole that gave some kind of trouble shot to the green. I punched a six-iron or maybe a seven-iron down low and cut it so that it rolled onto the green and went in the hole for a two.

Mark Triggs also won the 1973 Cherokee Country Club Invitational in Jacksonville. It was always a good tournament on a fun, nine-hole course. Between A.J. and Mark, the Triggs family won a bunch of barbecue tournaments and totaled four at Briarwood. While A.J. remained an amateur and built a successful insurance business, Mark tried a couple of times for his PGA card but narrowly missed both times. He now is in the oil business in Houston.

Guy Cullins had an illustrious college career at the University of North Texas in the late 1960s and early 1970s. The son of a golf pro and course superintendent, Austin Cullins, Guy played out of Willow Brook Country Club in Tyler for several years when his dad was in charge of course maintenance. He came close to winning at Briarwood in 1970 but could not overcome a red hot David Montgomery that year.

Cullins commented:

I always thought Briarwood was the Masters. I got into the final group one year and David Montgomery beat me... The cool thing about the barbecue deals was to get in the last group where there would be 80 golf carts back behind you. Everybody had their own cart and they liked to follow you. All of the barbecue circuit deals had a Calcutta and every time you played, the person who bought you would come out and follow you. They would say things like, "you know you have made a couple of bogeys and you need to make some birdies so I can get my money back on you." Or maybe more like, "just relax, make a few birdies, and I'll get my money back." That's what I remember.

In the late 1960s and early 1970s, the pro at Briarwood was Paul Hendrix. A delightfully upbeat guy who helped recruit the good players to the tournament, Hendrix doesn't recall a legendary story about one fine amateur who was just a little cocky in his college days.

Among the top college players recruited during the mid to late 1960s by Hendrix were Dallas' Chip Stewart and Jacksboro's Rik Massengale of the University of Texas, who could challenge a powerhouse University of Houston team led by two-time state am champion Hal Underwood of Del

Rio and the always tough John D. Mahaffey of Kerrville. All of these top players would play at Briarwood and never win.

Always clad in resplendent attire, one of the college hotshots found the barren and hard sand rough on the right side of the 5th hole, par-five that was a tight drive before a short iron to a blind green. It was a great little hole even if not out of the playbook of Ross or Tillinghast.

The 5th hole was also the furthest point from the clubhouse and the hotshot found his ball in the rough with a burrowing animal hole close by and affecting his stance. He called for a ruling and summoned Hendrix from the golf shop for a lengthy jaunt to the location of the ball. After looking at the ball and burrowing animal hole, Hendrix ruled that a free drop was allowable. The young player said thanks but that on second thought, he would just play it as it was.

Then, as the legend goes, the hotshot cold shanked his short iron over a barbed wire fence out of bounds. "Now you can drop it," Hendrix said. "Two club lengths, no closer to the hole."

It was on that same 5th hole in 1978 that Jimmy Wheeler of Dallas finally won in sudden death over Steve Bowman of Tyler. It was a good win by Wheeler, who later moved to Tyler and has made his home there since, but a tough blow to Bowman and the Briarwood members. Bowman's father Jewell was a longtime member and no member or member's son ever won the tournament in its 24 year history.

There were other Briarwood members to come painfully close, especially Mike McKinney in 1968, losing in a playoff to Arnold Salinas of Dallas.

The Classic Playoff

"Go back and tell him that I can bogey the last three or four holes."

Arnold Salinas

Dallas, Texas

It was going to be the classic match-up in the sudden death playoff to determine the winner of the 1968 Briarwood Invitational. It would be the local high school hero who was playing the golf of his life versus the smooth and dapper Dallas hustler who was just out of the service.

Or was it? While the high school star nervously pounded balls on the range under the watchful eye of his father, readying himself for the biggest moment of his young life, a mild commotion was taking place in the far corner of the putting green near the clubhouse.

Arnold Salinas was engaged in a stressful conversation with a couple of older men. For someone seemingly never ruffled, the distinctly handsome Salinas seemed mildly upset as sweat beads glistened over his dark eyebrows. His expensive golf shirt was slightly hanging out in back. A man of impeccable dress, Salinas showed the wear and tear of an already long afternoon.

Despite the apparent seriousness of the conversation, the Dallas golfer kept his voice muted as he continued the discussion. As was his style as a golfer, Salinas was determined to have his way in this dispute and the older men did not seem to like it. Whatever the proposal, the men all finally agreed on the solution.

It wasn't hard to figure out that the Calcutta split was probably the topic of conversation. Salinas had arrived as an unknown and sold low in the Calcutta. But he came with friend and fellow hustler Dick Martin and so knew how to negotiate a bet or a percentage of a Calcutta.

"I heard they are arguing over the Calcutta split," a man holding a beer announced to whoever might be listening. "Salinas told them that he wanted first and second combined for a split or he wasn't playing."

By this time, the 18-year-old Mike McKinney was raring to go. He had hit all the balls he needed to hit while his dad, Grady Faulk, sought to keep him calm. Finally there was an agreement between Salinas and his buyer. As everyone raced to the first tee, the debonair Salinas, a man of Latin descent, retrieved a sleeve of new balls and plopped them down to stroke a few putts and engage his mind for the task ahead.

With short, curly blond hair tucked under his trademark bucket hat, McKinney seemed plucked from a Norman Rockwell painting. He waited nervously for Salinas to arrive at the first tee for the coin toss by Briarwood head pro Paul Hendrix. Salinas finally trudged down the hill to the first tee and insisted that McKinney call the coin toss.

McKinney correctly called heads and was given the honor to hit first. The partisan home crowd gave a loud whoop in support of their local prodigy. "Go get him Mike," someone yelled at the top of their lungs.

Doffing his hat ever so slightly, McKinney placed his peg in the ground of the home course he had played so many times over the years as he learned the game. The first hole at Briarwood was a long and straight par-five with trees and loose sand lining the fairway on both sides. Since the fairway slanted from left to right, the perfect drive was a slight draw down the left side that would kick forward and run with the ball ending up in the center or right center of the fairway. The gallery of 200 or so people loved the natural amphitheater behind the first tee.

McKinney took dead aim and fired a low drawing tee shot right down the middle to the delight of the gallery. An adrenaline rush obviously helped with the distance as the ball skipped along the fairway and came to rest 270 yards from the tee. He was juiced up and had hit the ball 20 yards longer than normal.

Appearing totally unfazed, Salinas complimented his young opponent, pegged his own ball and several warm-up swings to loosen his muscles. Unlike McKinney, he had not hit a single shot on the practice tee before the playoff.

Salinas hit a solid drive as well but it started a good bit to the right of center and headed toward the right rough. A slight draw kept the ball from reaching the trees but Salinas had a slightly difficult shot from the light rough though his ball was still on grass and not in the loose sand.

Another whoop, aided by excitement and beer, was bellowed as the two combatants began their walk down the fairway among the late afternoon shadows. A small army of golf carts motored down the hill and onto both sides of the fairway. There was a silent collective agreement that this was indeed going to be good, going to be fun.

Although almost everyone in the crowd was for the local boy, Salinas did have his small contingent of supporters from his home course of Tenison Park in Dallas. *T Park* was known for heavy gambling action among its regulars and none of those were more colorful than the Beasley brothers, Leroy and Charles, who walked alongside Salinas as he approached his tee shot.

It was difficult to believe that Leroy and Charles were actually brothers since they did not look anything alike. Leroy was short and stocky with sandy brown hair and an obvious beer gut while Charles was tall and tanned with well-oiled black hair and a beer seemingly permanently attached to his right hand. He was a fun guy while Leroy was a worrier.

"Just keep it steady Arnold and the kid will fold," Leroy said. "Don't get greedy and lay-up on this hole because it doesn't help that much to get real close. Make the kid make the mistake."

Charles looked over at his shorter brother and shook his head. Both were decent golfers but inferior in ability and judgment to Salinas. The beer was having its way with Leroy's tongue.

"Hey, hey, guys," Salinas' caddy said. "My man knows the situation and he can handle it just fine."

The Beasley brothers were thus muted and remained motionless except for sips of beer. Salinas selected an iron and hit a good shot but just past a tree in the right side of the fairway, 130 yards short of the green. It seemed as though he played just the shot Leroy had suggested.

Salinas' ball had barely landed when the crack from McKinney's three-wood was heard and his ball scooted all the way down the left side of the fairway to within 50 yards of the green and on a slight upslope. The first green at Briarwood had a severe slope from back to front so downhill putts were hard to stop. It was a classic example, perhaps extreme, of what Brandel Chamblee later described as "pushed up greens." In other words, building the greens was simplified by shoving the earth up from front to back to create the putting surface. But the green also sat atop a large hill so any shot short of the green would not bounce up but instead roll back down some 10 yards short of the surface. With that in mind, Salinas hit his third too strong onto the back fringe, 25 feet from the hole.

Recognizing an opportunity, McKinney played his short pitch to about four feet but adjacent to the hole instead of below it so he would have a severe right to left breaking putt. Still, the local boy looked in control at this point.

"I thought I had him then for sure," McKinney said, recalling the match more than 40 years later. "It was going to be a very tough up and down or two putt from that back fringe. But then he lags it down there just a foot or so below the hole for a sure par and I have to decide to go for it or just try to lag it in. I didn't give it enough and we halved the hole."

The second hole was a sharp dogleg left down the hill and then back up a hill to a two-tiered green. McKinney again found the fairway while Salinas hit another drive to the right, this time into the trees. The rough on the second hole was firmer sand and Salinas was able to get his ball just short of the green with his second shot. McKinney then hit a thin short iron over the green. The advantage now seemed in Salinas' favor.

McKinney's chip from behind the green rolled about 20 feet past the hole and Salinas chipped up close. It looked like a done deal for Salinas until McKinney rolled in the long par putt and the crowd went nuts.

"I remember asking my dad, 'where did all of these people come from?'" McKinney said. "Until that moment, I had no idea that there were that many people following us. I guess I was in the zone or something."

The third hole was another par-five, long but straight downhill on the tee shot. Again McKinney found the fairway with extra length due to the moment and Salinas hung his tee shot to the right.

"I was still not where I wanted to be with my ball striking since I was just out of the service," Salinas said as he probed his memory. "But my chipping and putting was good enough to carry me. I was always a good chipper and putter going back to my days as a boy at Stevens Park in Dallas."

It was at Stevens Park that Salinas learned to play when his father would take him to the course. For two years, Salinas did nothing but putt while his dad played in his weekend game. Later, Salinas became good friends with Lee Trevino and the two played Tenison Park a lot. Salinas said:

Lee was a much better ball striker but I could stay close to him because of my short game. He would hit 16 greens and I would hit about 12 and we would shoot about the same score. But I went into the service and he went on to become Super Mex.

Salinas caught a tree on his second shot from the right rough and advanced his ball only a short distance past McKinney's drive. "I thought I had him again," McKinney said.

Both hit three-wood shots down to within 100 yards of the green. McKinney played his third to the back of the green, some 20 feet from the hole while Salinas stiffed his fourth shot.

"My ball was quasi against the fringe so I just had to be careful and lag it down," McKinney said. "He made his short putt for par and I was able to tap in mine."

McKinney said that his nerves were just fine because he had experienced a bad moment of hand shaking on a short putt for par on his last hole of regulation. He said he told friends that he had never had that sensation before and could only surmise that muscle memory helped him make that three-foot putt.

Salinas finished after McKinney and could have won in regulation with a birdie on the short, par-five 18th hole but failed to get up and down from a green side bunker. Only a few holes earlier, Salinas, via Dick Martin, had approached his buyer in the Calcutta about how they would divvy up their winnings. The buyer, a beer distributor from Palestine, said it his money and he would divvy it up the way he wanted to at the end of play.

"I told Dick, 'go back over and tell him that I can bogey the last three or four holes," Salinas said. "I think that helped us get what we wanted."

So the playoff had now reached the most difficult hole on the golf course. The par-three fourth was 240 yards from the tips and that's exactly where the tees were placed that Sunday. A small pond fronted the green and there was a creek running off to the right just short of hard pan and trees. A miss to the left was no bargain with a fairly sharp slope away from the green and several trees to cause problems.

McKinney selected a driver and hit a good shot just short and to the right of the green. His ball carried to that spot with no roll. It left him with a pretty simple pitch shot from below the hole as the green had the typical back to front slope, though not as severe as the first hole.

Salinas again blocked his drive to the right and this time he was in jail. It took a while to find his ball as it could have found the small ditch and that would have ended his hopes. His ball, however, was on the hard pan in the trees about pin high to the hole. Salinas then hit a punched sand wedge to about 12 feet past the pin, a remarkable recovery shot!

McKinney remained cool and chipped just past the pin about three feet, leaving a putt that was short but with plenty of left to right break. Salinas' downhill 12-footer was even more difficult with a slight break from left to right.

Showing nerves of steel, Salinas curled his downhill putt into the cup. It was simply a great par on a very tough hole and just magnified the great short game of the Dallas hustler.

Obviously a touch rattled, McKinney jabbed his putt too firmly and missed. The match was over… just like that it was done. In a state of shock,

McKinney quickly raked back his putt and made the mulligan. That of course made the empty feeling worse. McKinney said:

> *I am not a good loser so I was not a happy camper and the walk back to the clubhouse was a long one. My only consolation was the money. I was able to sell the clubs that I won and got some Calcutta money, too. And I got all kinds of invitations to tournaments the rest of the summer. I guess I became a marquee player.*

For Salinas, the trip back to Dallas in Martin's Cadillac was no doubt a fun one.

"It wasn't until later, when I looked at all of the good college players who were in that field, that I realized what a big tournament I had won," Salinas said. "To have beaten guys like Hal Underwood, who must have sold for about $12,000 in the Calcutta, is something that makes me proud. He was a super player back then."

Troup and the Other Majors

This sports column appeared in the Tyler *Morning Telegraph*, Labor Day, 1976.

Times change and people must learn to adapt. With the adjustment to changing times come certain sacrifices. It's all a part of the game.

Thus with heavy thunder crackling about and the skies filled with needed rain, this author slowly faces reality.

For the first time in many years, the struggling columnist will not carry his golf game outside the Rose City Metroplex during the Labor Day weekend. He will not mingle with the carousing celebs at Hilltop Country Club in downtown Troup, site of the yearly festival entitled the Hilltop Invitational Golf Tournament.

The plight cannot be resolved.

On Friday, the day of qualifying for the medalist prize at Hilltop, there is high school football to be covered. And on Saturday, the first round of the 54-hole event, there is the CTT desk. The CTT desk involves the layout and headline writing for the Sunday edition of the Tyler Courier Times-Telegraph. *And the rhetoric mechanic pictured above is in the barrel, one senior editor calls it amateur night in the sports department.*

These are truly times which try men's souls.

There are golf tournaments and there are social events throughout East Texas during the summer months. Each event sports its own identity, but none asserts such a strong sense of individuality as the Hilltop gathering.

Whoops, the power just went off. Shift to the manual typewriters and carry on. Remain undaunted.

The golf tournaments in each East Texas hamlet usually double as the community's top social gathering of the summer. So the frivolity is unlimited, people have a good time.

The string of tournaments are known in some circles as the "Beer and Bar-B-Que Circuit" and Troup's Hilltop classic is the last of majors.

The author's first excursion to the rolling hills and red clay fairways of Hilltop CC was way back in the late 1960s. Those were the days. Days when yipped three-foot putts were nonexistent and negative thoughts rare.

The record books will show two third-place finishes at Hilltop at ages 15 and 16. But it was that first year, at age 14, when the author discovered the meaning of a cocktail hour.

The years rolled by. But every summer, time was taken away from goofing off to play at the Hilltop tournament. Sort of a religious commitment.

This year's tournament, the 27th at Hilltop, should be a great one. Golf course superintendent Charlie Hargraves has the greens at Hilltop in excellent condition. In the past, the greens have always had a lot of grass on them, but were spongy and grainy. This year, Hargraves has verticut the greens often enough to eliminate that sponginess and the ball rolls across the greens with ease.

The rains Monday and Tuesday have got to help the condition of Hilltop's fairways for the tournament. The Hilltop track does not have the luxury of fairway watering system and rainfall is always appreciated the week of the tournament. Hitting sand-wedge shots off of the hard-baked clay is not fun.

The field for the 1976 tournament will be a good one. Gene Nelson of Arp is back to defend his crown and is a tough man to beat at Hilltop. But Nelson can expect strong competition from Pete McCarty of Tyler, the tournament director, and Jerry Warren of

Tyler. McCarty and Warren teamed to win a two-man scramble back in July at Hilltop and are both familiar with the subtle idiosyncrasies of the course.

High school flash Brad Jones of Tyler will play, as will past winners J.O. Crosby and Richard Herrington of Jacksonville.

It will be a good tournament and you can bet the Troup folks will enjoy themselves. Having a good time at Hilltop is one thing that hasn't changed in 27 year.

During the 1950s, 1960s, and 1970s, there were also well established tournaments in towns such as Palestine, Jacksonville, Athens, and even tiny little Troup, about twenty miles south of Tyler. The man to beat in those tournaments was a short and debonair man who owned a car repair shop in Palestine but reportedly never once got any dirt underneath his fingernails. With a short and quick backswing and a "pop it" putting stroke with a bulls-eye blade, Leroy Rocquemore is reported to have won 18 of the barbecue tournaments during the 1950s and 1960s in East Texas.

He defeated Joe Conrad at Kilgore when Conrad was the top rated amateur in Texas in 1953, and had some memorable duels with John Mahaffey of Kerrville and the University of Houston during the late 1960s. Rocquemore was one of the older amateurs who played every day throughout the year and challenged the "flat belly" college golfers when they came to town for the annual invitational.

Rocquemore's home course, Meadowbrook Country Club of Palestine, had a creek that meandered through all nine holes and set up some dicey iron shots to tight pins on greens set next to the water. The holes had two sets of tees so that some played as par-fours on the front side and par-fives on the back, and other variations that involved holes as par-fours or par-threes.

In 1968, Rocquemore and Mahaffey were locked into a duel on the final day when they arrived at the 14th hole. Playing as a relatively short par-five of about 500 yards, Mahaffey reached the green in two with a drive off of an elevated bluff and a five iron approach that left a 10-foot eagle putt. Rocquemore had to lay up but then hit his patented low and hooked sand wedge onto the green and spun it back into the hole for an eagle. Not wanting to exert himself with a walk across the bridge to the green in the East Texas heat, Rocquemore asked Mahaffey if he minded getting his ball from the cup.

That needle didn't quite do the trick since Mahaffey prevailed with a two-stroke win. Mahaffey would go on to win on the PGA Tour and won the PGA Championship in 1979.

Whenever the East Texas beer and barbecue circuit is discussed, the name Billy Martindale is always mentioned. Now in Dallas and best known for designing Royal Oaks Country Club, the site of the 2010 Texas State Amateur, with Don January, Martindale grew up in Jacksonville and was a gifted athlete. He was the national junior skeet shooting champion at age 11. Once introduced to golf, he gave up shooting and soon was busting par on the nine-hole Cherokee Country Club. He won the Texas State Junior in San Antonio in 1956. Later he would lead Texas A&M to three straight Southwest Conference championships.

Martindale said:

I played in my first barbecue tournament when I was twelve. Those tournaments got really big starting in 1950 and there was somewhere to play every weekend from May through Labor Day. We didn't have to go off and travel anywhere to find good competition. I won tournaments in Jacksonville, Athens, Palestine, Nacogdoches, Lufkin, and even Troup. I bet you don't even know where Troup is but it was the Hilltop Invitational.

Of all of the tournaments Martindale listed, the Hilltop Invitational on Labor Day weekend is the only one that remains an individual competition.

The course in Troup is on land leased from the school district so that for years the seventh hole ran alongside the football stadium. The course had to be altered approximately twenty years ago to eliminate that particular hole but this year will mark its 61st consecutive year. A sign of the times, it has now been shortened from three to two days of competition.

At one of Martindale's first times to play Troup, he walked down the hill from the clubhouse to the first tee, only a lad of twelve pulling a cart. A well dressed and towering man awaited him there.

"Are you caddying for someone," the friendly man asked.

"No, I am playing and I am gonna beat you mister," was Martindale's tart reply.

And Martindale did beat the large and athletic man who happened to be Guy V. Lewis of nearby Arp. Lewis would go on to fame as the basketball coach at the University of Houston, the fraternity president of *Phi Slamma Jamma*.

"It was a lot of fun," Martindale said of his days on the East Texas circuit. "I remember buying me a new 1957 Ford hardtop convertible to drive to college my freshman year."

With Calcutta money?

"Let's not go that far," Martindale said. "But there were times a guy might slip you $500 or so if you won."

More than the money, it was the competition and youthful memories that Martindale cherishes. Memories of people like Paul Peters, the Falstaff beer distributor in Tyler who had one of the few golf carts available in the early days, albeit a three-wheel model. Peters was a regular and loved to sip his favorite beverage and chomp his stogie while watching the terrific golf of Martindale and others on the beer and barbecue circuit.

"I can see those guys right now," Martindale said with a lilt in his voice. "It's enough to bring tears to my eyes."

Billy Martindale of Jacksonville, circa 1950's

The Calcutta Crooner

"There wasn't a dry eye in the crowd."

A.J. Triggs

Tyler, Texas

It was another hot and sticky summer night when the Calcutta concluded at the Meadowbrook Invitational in 1948. People didn't especially want to go home so they milled around outside with drinks in hand, talking about the tournament and the upcoming events of the weekend. They had enjoyed a nice barbecue dinner and marveled at the amount of money wagered in the Calcutta. Times were good. The oil business was going strong and everyone seemed happy and optimistic on the heels of the American victory in World War II.

As expected, defending champion Earl Stewart, just about unbeatable in those days, sold for the most money that evening. He would have to win the tournament to return a profit for his buyers but that never deterred them. Men like Red Bankston of Dallas had money and would pay to see if anyone could beat their man.

All of a sudden a strong and resonant voice could be heard above the din of the crowd. Someone was singing a popular Bing Crosby song and doing a fine job. He was singing a capella to a group of golfers. It was the Irish ballad *Tura Lura Lura* and the mystery singer's voice sounded even better than Crosby's. Was it the alcohol, the atmosphere, or was he really that good?

Spellbound and hanging on every note, a hush soon fell over the gathering as those listening intuitively knew this was a moment to be savored. Once the song was over, there was applause as people wondered who the singer was. Was he one of the golfers?

In attendance that night was an 18-year-old kid who had just graduated from high school and was playing in his first invitational tournament. He liked to sing himself and so recognized the brilliance of the performance.

That young boy was A.J. Triggs, who traveled to Kilgore from Dallas and went on to defeat Skinny Garrison of Nacogdoches to win the second flight. He took home a leather suit bag and "felt like I had won the U.S. Open." It marked the beginning of an amateur career that would later include playing on an NCAA championship team at the University of North Texas and winning his share of championship flights in the various barbecue events in East Texas.

Hearing that song in Kilgore 63 years ago remains one of Triggs' favorite memories of the beer and barbecue circuit. "I can still smell the barbecue and beer as if it was yesterday," Triggs said. "They had a big tent near the first tee and after the Calcutta the first evening, on Friday night, I remember Don Cherry singing *Tura Lura Lura*. There wasn't a dry eye in the crowd."

The singer was indeed Don Cherry the golfer who was already a top amateur but rarely came to East Texas. Instead, he preferred to play in the West Texas tournaments closer to his home in Wichita Falls. But the large Calcutta at Kilgore lured him east of the Trinity River. He also played that summer at the Premier Invitational just outside of Longview.

One of those rare individuals supremely gifted in two areas, Cherry was a product of a broken home during the depression. His father left home when he was still a small child and Cherry was devoted to his mother who worked and took in sewing to support her family. He vowed early on that he would never take a drink of alcohol or smoke a cigarette and has kept that vow. He developed his singing talents at church while learning golf as a caddy at the local golf course. He won the city junior and was on his way.

Cherry likes to point out that he has never had a lesson in golf or in singing. Yet he has excelled at both.

Serenading the golfers in Kilgore that night was just a prelude to being the only person ever asked to sing from the steps of the clubhouse of the Royal and Ancient Golf Club in St. Andrews. It was after the conclusion of the 1955 Walker Cup that the Americans won and Cherry chose the song, *I Believe*. It was well received by the huge gallery and he received praise for both his golf and his singing from the British sportswriters the next day.

Later, in the 1960s, Cherry was a regular guest on the *Dean Martin Show*, one of the more popular television shows of that time. His top selling record was *Band of Gold* in the late 1950s but his biggest monetary success came from singing the jingle for the Mr. Clean commercials.

Perhaps his greatest compliment as a singer was that all of the big stars like Crosby, Frank Sinatra, and Perry Como wanted Cherry to sing their songs before they went into the studio for recording. They wanted to see how he "treated" the song. In other words, he is a singer's singer.

Cherry never won the Meadowbrook Invitational as his bid in 1948 was derailed by the red hot play of Buster Reed from Dallas. Reed also defeated Stewart that year to win the championship.

In spite of his lack of success in East Texas, Cherry's golfing resume is impressive. He won the Canadian Amateur in 1953, the Sunnehanna Amateur in 1954 and played on three Walker Cup teams. He also played in numerous Colonials and Masters. His closest brush with golf greatness was finishing in a tie for ninth with Ben Hogan at the 1960 U.S. Open. Played at Cherry Hills in Denver, Cherry finished four shots behind winner Arnold Palmer and three behind the runner up Jack Nicklaus. Going into the final nine holes in 1960, Cherry was actually leading the tournament.

At the Masters one year, he was booked to sing at a local nightclub in Augusta that he did not realize was actually a strip tease joint. He was called on the carpet the next day by Clifford Roberts who ran the tournament with an iron fist during its early days.

Cherry explained:

He said they had never had anyone playing in their tournament sing at one of those places. And I just told him that I knew all of the other players and none of them had much of a voice. He was not amused but Bobby Jones got a kick out of it. But Mr. Jones told me to not give that answer the next time.

Now 87, Cherry no longer plays much golf but he sings professionally on occasion. His voice is still remarkably strong as he demonstrated last December at a special show in Houston. He is married to Francine, a former Broadway performer, and they live in Las Vegas. He has a website (doncherry.us) for those wishing to order his songs.

As for that match between Stewart and Reed in the finals in 1948, Triggs still vividly remembers some of the details. "At that time, Earl had to win the tournament to make money for whoever bought him in the Calcutta," Triggs said. "And invariably he did just that. He was good and he was cocky."

Reed, though not as well known at the time as Stewart, did not lack for confidence. He was teammates with Billy Maxwell who would win at Meadowbrook in 1949, and Don January at North Texas.

Triggs said of Reed and Stewart:

They were just alike and at the top of their games. I remember Buster hitting a 60 or 70 yard wedge shot up for a gimme on the fourth hole, a par-five, with Stewart off to the right in waist high Johnson grass. So Earl walks all the way up to the green and backhands the ball back to Buster. We all played match play in those days. Then he goes back to his ball and makes this vicious cut. His shot ends up closer than Buster's was. But Buster went on to win that match and the tournament.

Stewart would later become the only man to ever win a PGA Tour event on the same course where he was the club pro when he won the 1961 Dallas Open at Oak Cliff Country Club. Reed also played the tour, rooming with none other than Arnold Palmer in the early 1950s. He was later a much loved club pro and course owner in Jacksonville, Florida, before his death in 2007.

The Calcutta Crooner, Don Cherry, right, with Tommy Bolt circa the late 1950s

The Mysterious Mr. X

"I've got a long way to go to catch Miller Barber."

Tom Kite

Austin, Texas

Ask Miller Barber what he remembers most about his days on the beer and barbecue circuit and he quickly points to a match that he lost. A match in which it seemed every hole was birdied. It was in the finals of the 1957 Meadowbrook Invitational.

Barber came back to Kilgore the following year and won the 1958 title. A plaque on number eight is dedicated to him because of his length off the tee in the technological stone-age of persimmon woods and soft rubber balls. Later he became known as *Mr. X*, or just *X* for short, and won tournaments frequently on both the PGA Tour and the Champions Tour. But in 1957 he ran into a buzz saw from Dallas. He ran into Dick Whetzle.

For the record, Whetzle shot a 10-under-par 62 that day and it remains the competitive course record at Meadowbrook.

A first team All America golfer for the University of North Texas in 1958, Whetzle became a top club professional in Maryland. In 2000, he was inducted into the Middle Atlantic PGA Hall of Fame as both a player and an administrator. Whetzle teamed with Barber in the Texas Cup as an amateur in the late 1950s when their side defeated a pro team that consisted of Ben Hogan and Byron Nelson. Later he played in four U.S. Opens and two PGA Championships.

John Paul Cain of Sweetwater competed against Whetzle in college and described him thusly. "There was a guy named Dick Whetzle. Razzle, dazzle, diamond Dick Whetzle. He came out of the service and could really play."

He certainly dazzled *Mr. X* and the gallery that day in 1957. But that loss to Whetzle was a rare time that Barber played well and lost. He won his share of barbecue tournaments and then on the PGA Tour. He was the winner of the first Byron Nelson Classic when it changed its name from the Dallas Open and moved from Oak Cliff Country Club to Preston Trail Golf Club in 1968.

Barber grew up in Texarkana, Texas, and went to Texas High where he played football for a legendary coach of that time, Watty Myers. He tried out for the Arkansas Razorbacks but soon learned that he should stick to golf.

"I first met Miller in 1960 at the Odessa Pro-Am," Masters champion Charles Coody said. "I heard that he tried out for football at Arkansas but after one play he got up from the pile and was looking out of one of the ear holes in the helmet. That probably helped him decide to stick to golf."

Barber's athleticism is unquestionable when one looks at his swing and then sees the results. It's a funny looking swing that had a loop with his right elbow flying way out from his body but the ball invariably goes where he is looking. Like another Texan, Bruce Lietzke, Barber probably doesn't care what it looks like. Lietzke has said that he never wants to see his swing on film and it is doubtful if *Mr. X* looks at a lot of video.

Just how Barber got his famous nickname is not known but most think it is because of his quiet demeanor and love of privacy. It is said that nobody knew much about him during his early days on tour except that he could play and liked it just fine behind aviator sunglasses. Another guy who wore shades all of the time in the 1960s on tour was George Knudson of Canada, a great student of the golf swing who once made the statement, "I want it flawless."

One year Knudson was spotted in the Colonial clubhouse, sitting alone in the corner and sipping Scotch. When asked why he wore his shades at night, Knudson replied, "It's quiet back here." The same could probably be said of *Mr. X*.

Barber later became a co-owner with Read Omohundro of the Woodlawn Country Club in Sherman. It was at Woodlawn that Barber showed the most emotion that his *Mr. X* persona would allow. After blowing a sizable lead to lose the 1969 U.S. Open at the Champions Club, Barber returned home to Sherman where the people at Woodlawn held an elaborate banquet honoring him. It was okay to shed a tear or two because there was so much love in the room that night. But typical of Barber and Omohundro, disappointment did not deter them from enjoying an evening of good wine, good food, and lots of good jokes.

It was during a casual nine holes in front of scores of members in 1971 that Barber revealed his dry sense of humor. Playing with Sale Omohundro, Reed's son and then a high school senior, Barber hooked his opening tee shot and found it dead up against a tree.

"That's a tough way to start a round," one of the members said.

"No problem," Barber replied as he kicked the ball out into the fairway.

From that point, *Mr. X* proceeded to shoot a foot-wedge aided 29 or 30 for the nine holes. The gallery was more than appreciative but it was just a way to unwind for Barber while off the tour for a week. He was gracious with the younger Omohundro's two visiting friends who made up the foursome, giving them free tips to help their game.

When he hit the Champions Tour in 1981, Barber went on a tear, winning 24 times with three of them being U.S. Senior Opens. He and friend Don January dominated the Champions Tour that first decade.

Perhaps Barber's most enduring quality is stamina. He won the longest PGA Tour event ever played, The World Open in 1974 at Pinehurst, a 144-hole event. He beat Ben Crenshaw by three strokes. That win was an indication of what was to come since *X* has now played in 1,293 PGA Tour and Champions Tour events.

When Tom Kite was congratulated last year at the Texas Golf Hall of Fame ceremonies for reaching the 1,000 starts milestone for both tours, he said thanks but added, "I have a long way to go to catch Miller Barber."

Barber's record for the most starts makes him the Lou Gehrig of golf. It could be broken one day, as Gehrig's record in baseball was by Cal Ripken Jr., but life has to be very kind to that person.

Top: The Cupit brothers from the left: Bobby, Jacky, Buster and David.
Bottom: Buster and Jacky shaking hands with Arnold Palmer and Jack Nicklaus at the 1966 PGA Team Championship.

The Cupits

"Buster called me one day and said he shot his age. He was 58."

Chris Cupit

Atlanta, Georgia

Druid Hills Golf Club is located in the beautiful and leafy neighborhood near downtown Atlanta. It's in the heart of Georgia where much of the movie *Driving Miss Daisy* was filmed. It is an old and stately club with an immaculately maintained course that is the annual site of the Dogwood Invitational, a top amateur competition with a national field of college-age players. In the late 1990s, the name Chris Cupit was near the top of the leaderboard. When a Texas native sees the name Cupit, it is a given that the trail leads back to Longview and East Texas golf.

An accomplished amateur in Atlanta, Chris is the son of the late David Cupit. David was a highly respected golf pro in Atlanta who started the Rivermont Golf Club in an Atlanta suburb during the 1970s. It is still owned and operated by Chris and the Cupit family. Chris is also the current president of the Georgia Golf Association. And yes, David was one of the eight Cupit boys from just outside of Longview.

Prominent for years in East Texas golf, the Cupit name evokes memories of great performances. Jacky was a top amateur who was virtually unbeatable on the East Texas barbecue circuit during the late 1950s and early 1960s. He turned pro in 1962 and won three times on the PGA Tour before injuries slowed his career. His older brothers Buster and Bobby won their share of barbecue tournaments during the 1940s and 1950s.

David was the fifth of the eight brothers and moved to Atlanta. He was tragically injured in a hunting accident in the mid 1980s and lived twenty years confined to a wheelchair before dying in 2007.

At Druid Hills Golf Club that day, David was watching Chris play. Although Chris did not have a good final round, he still finished in the top ten against his younger opponents. Chris played college golf at the University of Virginia and had tour potential, but like Buster, opted for a more settled life off of the road. Buster, the third oldest of the Cupit brothers, has run the Longview Country Club for forty years now and Chris remembers a funny conversation from years ago.

"I was talking with Buster and he mentioned that he had recently shot his age so I said 'what did you shoot,' thinking something in the mid to high 60s," Chris said. "But he said 58. He said it as if it was just another good round. Yes, he can play some golf."

Buster is now 85 but still active in the day-to-day operations at his course and plays at least three days each week. He regularly shoots his age and though Longview Country Club is not a difficult course, as Dan Jenkins once wrote about the old Premier course outside of Longview, "it is not the easiest course designed by man."

Working for Buster in the golf shop of Longview Country Club, Butch Kane said, "He must have shot his age more than anyone because he does it every time he plays."

Buster emphasized that he needs to shoot better than his age. "If I shoot my age then I'm going to lose some money," Buster said. "I usually shoot anywhere between 66 and 74 on most days now."

In the clubhouse of the Longview Country Club is a picture of Buster and Jacky playing in the 1966 PGA National partnership tournament at West Palm Beach, Florida. Their playing partners were Arnold Palmer and Jack Nicklaus.

"That's pretty good company," Buster said. "We finished fifth but played in the same group with them during the final round."

Jacky described his third round that year as one of the best he ever played on the tour.

That four-ball at West Palm Beach followed the Cajun Classic that year when I won it. Buster and I were leading after three days. I set a course record on Saturday. I made eleven birdies and shot 63 with a double bogey. I was so confident with my driver that I flirted too closely to a lake and the ball trickled in. That hole hurt us because it was bogeyed by Buster.

Now the pro at the Links at Land End near Yantis, Jacky's other accomplishments on the tour were wins at the Western Open at Medinah in Chicago in 1962 and at the Canadian Open during his rookie year in 1961, where Buster finished second.

"I won the Canadian Open my rookie year in 1961 and Buster finished second. I am not sure if that has ever happened before or since, brothers finishing first and second in a tournament," Jacky said.

The near miss of winning the U.S. Open in 1963 by Jacky is etched into the memories of those old enough to have been watching the final round on television, black and white TV for most. Cupit had about an eight-foot putt to win and lipped out. The miss forced a three-way playoff the next day at The Country Club in Brookline just outside of Boston. He lost to Julius Boros as did Palmer, the third player.

Buster has his own unique U.S. Open memory. It occurred in 1957 at the Inverness Golf Club in Toledo, Ohio.

I played with this 17-year old kid the first two days. I told my wife that I traveled all this way to play in the U.S. Open and they pair me with a young boy. Well, that young boy turned out to be Jack Nicklaus and after those two rounds, I told my wife that if he keeps his desire, there is no telling what he will accomplish.

Both Buster and Jacky are known for their devotion to drawing the ball from right to left. Master champion Charles Coody of Abilene said he was always impressed with Jacky's ability to play the hook so consistently well.

"For me, I just naturally hooked everything from my driver down to my putter," Buster said. "So I stayed with it and still do."

Bobby, the next oldest after Buster, was also a good player who won some barbecue tournaments, most notably the Willow Brook Invitational in Tyler in the late 1950s. There were two brothers older than Buster, Homer and Vernon, who, like David, died in 2007. The other two brothers, Jerry and Freddy played golf but not competitively.

The Cupit clan also includes two sisters, Bonnie and Mary. All ten of the children grew up across the street from a public golf course and just down the street from the Premier Refinery golf course that was the site of the Premier Invitational where Homero Blancas shot his famed 55.

Jacky is the youngest of the boys. Mary, like David, moved to the Atlanta area. "I visited Chris in Atlanta one time and he had some pecans in his backyard that were very good," Jacky said. "They reminded me of the pecan orchards near Winona that Sylvester Dayson (the Premier Refinery owner) once owned."

Just like the Cupits, when there is talk of pecans, the trail leads back to East Texas.

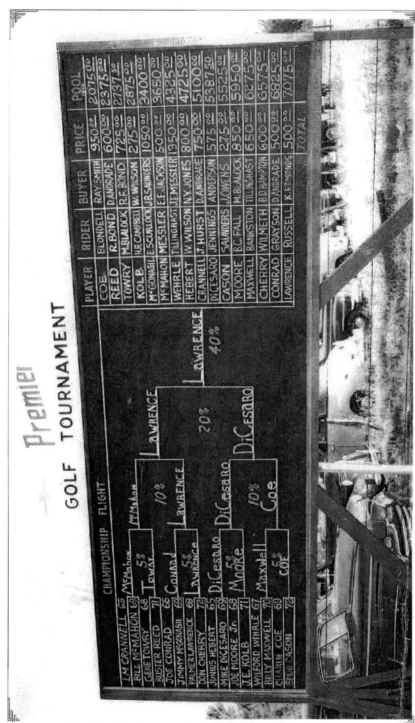

The Calcutta board at the 1948 Premier Invitational

The Calcutta Board At Premier

"He (Coe) went up to Rochester, New York, the next week and won the U.S. Amateur."

Billy Maxwell

Jacksonville, Florida

Dennis Walters is now known around the world as one of golf's greatest ambassadors. Seated in his special wheelchair, Walters loves to entertain fans at PGA Tour events. He can hit the ball solid and long with just his arms and has fun with his sidekick, adorable dog Benji Hogan.

Walters played on the beer and barbecue circuit in East Texas when he ran around with fellow North Texas golfers Guy Cullins, Rip Collins, and Hale Baugh. He was tall and lean and could really hit the ball long in those days, even with the soft balls and the persimmon drivers.

Preparing for the PGA Tour qualifying school, Walters was injured in a cart accident when only in his early 20s. That he has overcome misfortune to become a prominent example of determination and spirit is inspirational to all golfers and others who may not even play the game.

When Walters first saw the old Calcutta board from the 1948 Premier Invitational, he was beside himself. "This is awesome, just awesome," Walters said from his South Florida home. "This Calcutta board just blows me away. To see all of those names from back then at that little course in East Texas is just amazing."

Calling the Premier nine-hole track little is an understatement. It was truly tiny but not easy. That is evident by the scores posted by some of the top amateurs in the country. Walters was quick to point out that the board has two U.S. Amateur champions, a British Amateur champion and a PGA Championship winner on it. And none of those guys ended up winning.

Reading down the list it is fascinating to see what each golfer represented in the late 1940s or early 1950s. No one is sure as to the exact date of the photo, but the money listed would be roughly equivalent to $250,000 in today's currency. That's a nifty little amateur tournament and we have to say amateur with a little wink.

- L.M. Crannell – They call him *Luscious Lucious* and he was a member of the University of North Texas golf team coached at that time by Fred Cobb. His teammate Billy Maxwell was also playing but Crannell had a 65 in the qualifying round to Maxwell's 70. He lost to Bill McMahon of Longview in the first round but Crannell had an impressive amateur resume while at North Texas. A native of Dallas' Oak Cliff area, his biggest win was the Trans Mississippi Amateur in 1951. He lost in the finals of the 1951 Premier Invitational to East Texan Raleigh Selby, another legend of the beer and barbecue circuit.

- Bill McMahon – Now in his 90s and still living in Longview, McMahon no longer plays golf but won his share of events in East Texas through the years. His locker at Pinecrest Country Club is intact and will soon be preserved for its members to see, much like Ben Hogan's at Shady Oaks Country Club in Fort Worth.

- Gene Towry – Another UNT player, Towry was small but tough as nails. He would later win the national public links championship in 1969 when it was played at Tenison Park in Dallas, not far from where he grew up.

- Buster Reed – This was one of the most beloved of all of the UNT golfers who defeated Earl Stewart of Dallas in an epic match at the Kilgore Invitational. He was taken out early by Towry.

- Joe Conrad – Still sporting red hair in his early 80s, Conrad won the British Amateur in 1955 and can still recount almost every shot. As important as winning that major amateur competition was the Texas state junior played in Conrad's hometown of San Antonio. Back in those days, a junior could play in the state tournament until age 21 and Conrad kept playing at historic Brackenridge Park until he won the state junior at age 20.

- Jimmy McGonagil – A native of Texarkana, McGonagil was an accomplished amateur who was a good friend of Byron Nelson. He once defeated A.J. Triggs at the Four States Invitational at Texarkana Country Club and asked if he could give the young Triggs a few pointers. He told Triggs to check with Nelson before working on the small changes. When Triggs asked Nelson he was told that anything Jimmy McGonagil told him could be implemented without question. Still, he lost to Conrad in the first round.

- Palmer Lawrence – Knowing what we know now, what a great name for a golfer! Another Dallas guy, Lawrence won the tournament and probably went home with more money than he knew what to do with. About 10 years later, he would team with A.J. Triggs to play an exhibition match at Mineola Country Club against another North Texas State great, Benny Castloo and Nelson. It was during the Watermelon Festival at Mineola, a nice little nine-hole track on US Highway 80, the main east to west highway before Interstate 20. Lawrence and Triggs won the match but Nelson wowed the gallery by teeing up his first drive on a giant watermelon used as a tee marker. He busted the drive straight down the middle!
- Don Cherry – Could have easily won the U.S. Open at Cherry Hills in 1960 but stumbled home after playing partner Sam Snead told him as much. A unique man of many talents, most especially a singer's singer who had some top hits and would "treat" a song for some famous singers like Dean Martin, Bing Crosby or Perry Como. Played in the 1955 Walker Cup and partnered with the great amateur Harvie Ward during the matches that the USA won at St. Andrews.
- Junius Hebert – Better known as Jay Hebert and the winner of the PGA Championship in 1960. His brother Lionel won the PGA in 1957. He was a winner of nine tour events and also a Purple Heart recipient for being wounded during the battle of Iowa Jima in the South Pacific during World War II.
- Mike DiCesaro – Not much is known about this man except that the 1948 Longview newspaper said he was the Houston municipal champion that year and he knocked off a future PGA champion in Hebert, a fine San Antonio amateur in Joe Moore, and then a future two-time U.S. Amateur champion in Charlie Coe of Ardmore, Oklahoma. DiCesaro lost in the finals to Lawrence but was a bargain in the Calcutta and no doubt won his buyer and himself some spending money with the runner-up finish.
- Joe Moore, Jr. – the pride of San Antonio. Along with Joe Conrad, Moore came into the tournament touted as the winner of both the New Orleans and Baton Rouge invitationals that summer. Moore would come back and win at Premier in 1949.
- J.E. Kolb – an amateur from nearby Henderson who was a long shot to win like McMahon.
- Wilford Wehrle – a top amateur from Louisville, Kentucky, who lost in the finals of the 1946 Premier to Earl Stewart, Jr. Wehrle played in the 1935 Masters so he obviously had a lot of game for many years. He ran

into a buzz saw from Abilene in the first round, losing to Billy Maxwell. Wehrle sold for the most in the Calcutta.

- Billy Maxwell – an amateur from Abilene who didn't like to lose. He is reported to have won 34 straight tournaments at one point before turning pro. He still plays several times a week in Jacksonville, Florida, where he owns a golf course with former PGA Tour player Chris Blocker. Maxwell won six times on the PGA Tour and also claimed the 1951 U.S. Amateur.

- Charlie Coe – perhaps the best amateur of all time. He won two U.S. Amateurs, played in 19 Masters and finished tied for second in 1961. He lost in the finals of the U.S. Amateur in 1959 at the Broadmoor to a pudgy 19-year-old guy named Jack Nicklaus. He had a bet at Oklahoma City Country Club that he could shoot 68 or better and hook every shot except for putts. The next day he would make the same bet but fade every shot. He won those bets most of the time. There is now a prestigious amateur event named in his honor at the Broadmoor outside of Colorado Springs.

- Spud Cason – a Fort Worth golfer who had the misfortune to draw Coe in the first round.

Preacher's Boy

"He was a cute little boy with blond hair and his dad said he looked like a preacher's boy."

Rick Maxey

Tyler, Texas

Finding the farm is a chore but well worth the trouble. The Maxey Farm of Rick and Missy Maxey is just outside of Tyler near Lake Tyler. The charming farmhouse is framed by green hills as far as the eye can see. It's not the bluegrass of Kentucky but it's a close second.

Gliding along the long crushed-rock driveway attracts the attention of two gorgeous brown horses. Their coats glistening in the spring sunshine, the two thoroughbreds begin prancing alongside the car and stop near the end of the fence adjacent to the house. Appearing like twins, both fillies sport a broad white blaze down the front of their heads that are gently bobbing up and down.

Sitting on the front porch in a rocker is the still youthful looking Maxey. He has a beer on a table close by and is fidgeting with a wedge. A smile breaks out because the reason for the visit is to talk some golf.

Maxey is one of those beer and barbecue veterans who "gets it." He loves his golf and raising horses but he is more than that. Much like his good friend from Kilgore, Terry Stembridge, he loves history, especially when it pertains to golf and East Texas.

Start talking about all the good players in Texas, both now and more than 50 years ago, and Maxey will chime in with some good data. It may be in story form or he may pull out an article in an old paper or even rarer, a radio recording of a match between Earl Stewart, Jr. and Wilford Wehrle at the Premier Invitational in 1946. Maxey pulled $100 from his front pocket to get an old 78 rpm record converted to a compact disc. But now he has a treasure to add to his library.

The record and newspaper clippings from the late 1940s were the result of the generosity of Suzzette Shellmyer, whom Maxey visited on occasion near Winona. Mrs Shellmyer is the daughter of Sylvester Dayson, the former owner of Premier Refinery where the Premier Invitational was always contested.

Maxey has won his share of barbecue tournaments but, like most golfers, has come close but not won in many more. He still has the course record in Center, a 62 that included a 29 on the back nine. He finished second in Center in 1975 to an international phenom at that time, Jaime Gonzales of Rio de Janeiro, Brazil. Gonzales played at Oklahoma State during the 1970s and was quite an entertainer as well as a great player. He wowed some folks at the American Classic tournament at Longview's Pinecrest by saying and demonstrating that he could hit 10 bunker shots to within 10 feet of the hole in 10 seconds. Gonzales was kind of the Seve Ballesteros of the barbecue circuit in those days.

The Stephen F. Austin golf team that Maxey played on in the early 1970s was loaded with talent, no pun intended. Playing with Maxey were Ronnie Tallent of Austin, Terry Brown of Tyler, and John Lee Pigg of Center.

Maxey and Brown also won an unusual beer and barbecue tournament at Briarwood in the spring of 1971. It was a partnership tournament with the Calcutta small and secondary to the competition. It was a quality field with Maxey and Brown winning a playoff over the team of Dean Overturf and Ken Mossman of Dallas and Doug Tewell and Jim Shade of Oklahoma State. Also in that field was the team of Mark Hayes and Danny Edwards of Oklahoma State.

Growing up in the oil business in the Longview area, Maxey was seemingly raised to play quality golf by his father. A most likeable man, Preacher Maxey had those Popeye forearms that are often the trademark of good players for the simple reason that good golf requires a square clubface at impact and strong arms and hands sure help with that chore. Rick Maxey inherited those forearms and hands and even now, at age 62, can send the ball flying a long way off of the tee.

Preacher Maxey was one of those men from the early days of the barbecue circuit that is hard to forget. He passed away in 1992 but it is easy to recall his attributes. He had a quiet intensity that was allayed by a pleasant demeanor. His looks were straight out of a comic strip. He had huge forearms covered with white blond curly hair. Rick has inherited both the forearms and the quiet intensity.

"No one really knows how he got that name Preacher," Maxey said. "He was a cute little boy and his father said he looks like a preacher's boy."

Indicative of how Maxey has maintained his physical fitness is the gap of years between wins at the Meadowbrook Classic in Kilgore, a tournament that Stembridge still helps promote. Played at the Meadowbrook Country Club that was for a period of time named Roy H. Laird Country Club, Maxey won the event in 1974 and 1975 while just out of college and then won again 25 years later in 2000 and for a fourth time in 2008. He has hopes of winning a fifth championship before the distance off the tee begins to significantly wane.

Like most good players, including one his heroes from years gone by in East Texas, Raleigh Selby, Maxey knows the short game is a cure for many ills. So he has an area in front of his farm house to work on his chipping. Selby used to have a chipping and putting green in front of his home in nearby Overton. Selby won the Kilgore tournament in 1945, 1950, and 1964 and was known for playing all over the state and elsewhere with his good friend Leon Taylor of Tyler.

Like Selby, Maxey also dabbles in the oil business while raising his horses as a gentleman farmer. As he studies golf and how to get better at age 62, Maxey sees lots of similarities between horse racing and the game he loves.

Raising horses and playing competitive golf are actually very similar. You have to take both in phases, one step at a time. You can't raise a horse without being patient and all good players know that it is hard to get all 14 clubs going well at the same time. When I am getting ready for a tournament, I know when I am ready and when I am just kidding myself.

Hope springs eternal in all golfers and Maxey is no different. He plans to play some barbecue events in the summer of 2012 and would like to win one more time. He showed that he still has the right stuff with a round of 65 at The Cascades, the old Briarwood course redesigned some 10 years ago by Mark Hayes. The round included eight birdies and an eagle but also a double and three bogeys.

"It was a flash of good play but I know I am not ready to play in a tournament," Maxey said. "I still have to get sharp before the tournaments this summer but I am planning to give it a go. Until I begin to lose my distance off the tee, I will compete."

With that, Maxey turned his attention back to his horses. "Let's load up and go check on one of my horses that got kicked in the chest," Maxey said. "I need to attend to him and drain some fluid off his wound."

The little jaunt down the road toward Troup, a longtime site of a beer and barbecue tournament, was delightful. Maxey has two more parcels of nice farm land for his horses. Along with his helper, Maxey attends to the skittish animal that is enormous when examined from close range.

Heading back to his farmhouse, Maxey said he wants to take a slight detour and show me something. We arrive at his house only to circle it and head downhill some 300 yards or more to a small stall. After stopping the car, we walk to where a large mare is grazing. Close beside her is a scrawny looking colt lying in the grass with its legs all tangled up beneath it.

Suddenly the tiny horse pops up like a blow-up balloon and its shaky legs steady beneath it. The tiny horse is twitching and moving its head from side to side.

"That's a good sign," Maxey said with a grin. "When they are nervous like that it means they just may be able to really run. This horse is about 24 hours old."

Wow, what a sight! It is the beginning of a new life, the life of a beautiful animal. And the connection is obvious–hope springs eternal. One day the beautiful foal on the Maxey farm may win the Kentucky Derby and each spring marks the beginning of a new golf season for guys like Maxey who are still chomping at the bit.

Rick Maxey, left, with his father Preacher,
circa the mid 1980s

The Best Golfer Who Never Played

"I would just say that I had something else to do."

Ophel Caldwell

Tyler, Texas

To watch him hit practice balls was like watching Ben Hogan. Each shot was struck with precision and the balls all collected in a tiny circle some 150 yards away. He practiced at the East Texas Fairgrounds near Rose Stadium, where years later the legend of Earl Campbell would emerge. Now paved over, that field was one of a few places to practice with your own golf balls. Hit them all away and then pick them up. The turf at the fairgrounds wasn't great but it was tightly mown and you could hit every club, including your driver.

A funny incident occurred one day at the fairgrounds when as youngsters Mark Triggs and I were picking up balls we had already hit and a car rolled slowly by Mark's bag that was a long way away. The car stopped and a man picked up Mark's clubs and put them in the front seat before driving off. We started yelling and took off toward the car when it abruptly stopped and he fell out onto the ground literally rolling over and over laughing uncontrollably. When we weren't hitting or picking up our own balls, we were intently watching the action of this man that we liked so much.

Sometimes wearing a lid like Hogan's, his footwork was exquisite and so pronounced that his shoes were permanently altered in their shape. Not allowed on the private courses in those days, he played at Bellwood Golf Club. An 18-hole course that was in decent shape, Bellwood was an 18-

hole track crammed into acreage more suitable for nine holes. The course had common Bermuda grass greens and no sand traps with lots of trees and a creek that meandered throughout the course. Because it was tight with some water in play, the simple layout was easy but had some character. Only about 5,800 yards, low scores could be had if the ball was kept in play and the grainy greens putted well.

That said, the golfer who emulated Hogan would usually shoot under par and dipped as low as 64 on at least two occasions that I had the pleasure of playing with him. He had the controlled flight on his shots that are indicative of well struck shots. Unlike Hogan, he loved to play a draw on every shot, including those interpretive wedge shots that separate the good players from the impostors.

Having been introduced to golf as a young boy, he caddied for some of the best players at Willow Brook Country Club and then on the beer and barbecue circuit. He never played in any of the barbecue tournaments because of one problem.

Ophel Caldwell's complexion was too dark. Handsome in a way similar to boxer Cassius Clay (Muhammad Ali) of that same time period, he was capable of competing well in the local amateur tournaments but East Texas was not willing to embrace such a change in mores.

"Back then, if someone asked me why I wasn't playing, I would just say that I had something else to do," Caldwell said.

Born in Tyler in 1934, Caldwell was about 12-years old when he first caddied for Ralph Morgan at Willow Brook. Morgan stumped the young caddy when he said, "Give me a stick."

"I didn't know what to do," Caldwell said. "I kept looking for a stick because I didn't know golfers called their clubs sticks. Ralph laughed because he knew it was my first time to caddy."

Before turning 18 and joining the Army, Caldwell continued to caddy and was able to cobble together a set of clubs. All of the caddies in those days were young black kids and they would hide clubs and use them while the members weren't around. Caldwell said he might have a seven-iron hidden somewhere while another caddy had a five-iron stashed away and so on.

Then the day came in 1951 when Caldwell caddied in the same group as the great Hogan from Fort Worth. It was an exhibition round with Morgan and two top amateurs from Willow Brook. There was a large gallery following the group. It was an experience that Caldwell still remembers vividly today and one that changed his life because it created a deep admiration and awe for how a golf ball should be hit.

"I had seen some good players but nothing like that," Caldwell said. "The sound, the trajectory, it was different. And I think I just thought to myself, 'I want to be able to do that.'"

Caldwell said there was pressure to do a good job that day. "He had me tend the flag on the second hole and boy was I nervous," Caldwell added:

> He was putting from a long way out and lagged it up close… But what I remember more is the shot he hit on a par-five down in the low area of the course. I had never seen anyone hit a ball like that. It was a four-wood to a green that was guarded by trees and no one ever tried to hit it in two shots that I could remember. The sound of that shot is something I will remember the rest of my life. And I heard someone say loudly, "good God almighty."

Caldwell said he admired Hogan because he didn't imitate anyone's swing. "He built that swing and it held up for him."

Having become a topnotch caddie by that time in 1951, Caldwell caddied for L.M. Crannell, Jr. of Dallas in a couple of tournaments on the barbecue circuit. Crannell was one of the University of North Texas hotshots at that time, having won the City of Dallas junior championship before heading off to college and then winning the Trans Mississippi Amateur at Brook Hollow in Dallas in 1951, beating SMU's Don Addington in the finals.

"He was a super player," Caldwell said. "A great putter. We won the invitational at Athens and then was rolling along at the Premier tournament before losing to Raleigh Selby."

Selby beat Crannell in the finals that year but it wasn't the first time that Caldwell had seen the winner's game.

"Man, ole Raleigh Selby and Leon Taylor were tough in those days," Caldwell said. "You didn't want to play those two."

Not too long after seeing Hogan, Caldwell joined the Army and stayed in the service for 13 years. He was able to play golf while in the Army, mostly in Germany. He learned the game while in the service and competed in tournaments. He played at about the same time as Orville Moody and John Jacobs.

"I played in the same tournament as Moody once at Fort Riley, Kansas," Caldwell said. "I am not sure if he won it but I finished a good ways back. My best golf was in Germany when I won a Battalion tournament and then got to go to Berlin for the Division championship."

While on leave in 1962, Caldwell caddied for Jim Fetters of Port Arthur during the Briarwood Invitational in Tyler. Fetters led for three rounds but faltered during Sunday's final round with a 40 on the front nine.

The tournament was won by Dudley Wysong of McKinney who was an outstanding amateur who lost in the finals of the U.S. Amateur the year before to Jack Nicklaus at Pebble Beach. Wysong would later turn pro and won twice on the PGA Tour.

"Wysong was a super player," Caldwell said. "My brother Noel followed him that last day. Fetters told me that he had a dream or something the night before and that he lost the tournament. I think that threw him off."

After getting out of the service in 1965, Caldwell moved back to Tyler but never played in the Briarwood tournament or any of the other barbecue events in East Texas. No one told him that he couldn't play but it was kind of understood in those days. A gentleman and a truly gentle man, Caldwell didn't want to confront the double standard of that time. In that respect, he was somewhat like Teddy Rhodes of Nashville, who many say was actually a better player than Charlie Sifford but didn't want to go through the pressure of breaking the color line in pro golf during the 1950s and early 1960s.

So, in ways of temperament and style of play, Caldwell was much like Rhodes. He is not tormented by regrets of what might have been, preferring instead to enjoy life and recall his love of the game of golf.

"Today it wouldn't be a problem but it was just different back then."

Sage Advice

"Emmitt told me to just get out there and hit it and then walk away."

Gerald Joyce

Palestine, Texas

Gerald Joyce is 88 years old now and thinking about getting back on the golf course. A gifted athlete, Joyce has always enjoyed both golf and tennis. In recent years, he has played more tennis than golf.

The same was true some 70 years ago when Joyce was attending SMU on a tennis scholarship. His father was a charter member of Meadowbrook Country Club in Palestine when it opened in 1921 and always encouraged Gerry to play golf.

Joyce said:

> *I was on a tennis scholarship to SMU and back then you had to do some work for that. So every day I had to roll the clay courts on campus. I was living in the athletic dorm and would just take my wedge and shoot some balls along the way on the two blocks I walked to the courts. That helped my wedge game and the wedge was always my best club.*

In the summer of 1942, Joyce was only 18 years old when an older friend who loved golf, Emmitt Pryor, took him to his first beer and barbecue tournament in Tyler. It was not a glorious debut but provided a wonderful teaching moment that later served Joyce well in golf competition.

"I had been shooting about par at home but in qualifying, I played so bad that I was in the fifth flight," Joyce said. "It was the pressure, I guess, but I stumbled through (won) the fifth flight and the next week was the Kilgore tournament."

Joyce had to be talked into going to Kilgore by Pryor, who was encouraging but also gave the young golfer some free advice in the form of constructive criticism. He focused on how Joyce was to comport himself while playing a match. In those days, almost all of the competition was match play and thus gamesmanship was a big part of a golfer's arsenal.

"He said, 'Come on, let's go to Kilgore,'" Joyce said:

He said, "now I don't want you to talk to the other players because they will needle you. Just go out there and play it and see what you come up with..." I barely got into the Championship Flight with a 76 and then I got out there and played my first match. And Emmitt told me to "just get out there and hit the ball and walk away, get out of the way and don't listen to any conversation" and I did and stumbled through that one and won it. That was the first championship match that I won and I can remember those comments from Emmitt.

Joyce continued to follow Pryor's advice and advanced to the finals against the reigning club champion at Kilgore's Meadow Brook Country Club. Despite his adherence to the "no conversation" policy, Joyce was four down with six holes to play.

And I did just the same thing–hit it and take off. And I birdied the next four holes and drew even. I sank two long putts and got to 17 and lipped the putt for a birdie there. Then I hit my approach about 20 or 25 feet past the hole on 18... And I just got up there like I knew what I was doing and putted that stupid thing and it ran down there and would have gone off the green if hadn't hit the cup. But it hit the cup and fell in. I won the match.

To go from winning the fifth flight in Tyler to winning the championship flight in Kilgore certainly seems incomprehensible today but there are several things to consider before scoffing that it must have been a fluke. For starters, take a look at Joyce's record in the years to come. He won at Kilgore again in 1946 and also was runner-up two years at Meadow Brook in 1947 and 1948. He lost to Earl Stewart in 1947 and Buster Reed in 1948.

Joyce had to be reminded that he won at Kilgore a second time. Of the two loses in the finals, once prodded and then asked if he remembered those matches, Joyce deadpanned, "I'm afraid so, he was much better," about Stewart and, "I am trying to forget," about Reed. In other barbecue tournaments around East Texas, Joyce won his share. He beat Raleigh

Selby in the finals at Nacogdoches and Palestine in 1949 and also won at Palestine in 1950 and 1951.

One other factor to consider about going from the fifth flight to the championship flight in 1942 versus modern golf is all of the serious golf being played in the lower flights. Back in the day, the sage advice was to play in the first or second flight if your game wasn't quite championship caliber but don't make the mistake of getting in the third flight where you were apt to get your brains beat out.

1971 Masters Champion Charles Coody said:

Two things happened to hurt the old barbecue tournaments. The clubs started doing the best ball tournaments or two-man scrambles so that nobody wants to play an individual tournament anymore. People want to have a two or three handicap but not post a medal score or play in the Championship flight and lose a match 8 and 6. So the individual tournaments went by the wayside. So competitive golf with individuals is nonexistent and if there is one today, it is a novelty.

That may sound harsh but it is hard to argue with its truth. And speaking of losing a match so lopsidedly, it has happened to the best of them. A case in point is a Longview newspaper article about the 1946 finals match at the Pinecrest Invitational – *Earl Stewart, Jr. defeats Tommy Bolt, 10 and 8!* One would assume that was a 36-hole final, otherwise Stewart would have won 10 consecutive holes. Bolt, as many know, did not blossom until his mid to late 30s but won the U.S. Open at Southern Hills in Tulsa 12 years after the Longview shellacking.

As for Joyce, he remembers the Calcutta at the Kilgore tournament in 1942 and how a local businessman saved him from embarrassment. The minimum bid that night was $25 so Joyce's friend Pryor bid that so he would sell. Then a wealthy Kilgore man named Roy H. Laird bid $30.

They hollered around for about 10 minutes but I never got another bid. So I sold to Mr. Laird for $30. I don't know how much he made but he made something. He asked me, "What's your next tournament? Let me give you some money so you can go play there...." I think it was $50 or $75. That would be my guess but that was a bunch then. I went to the next tournament, somewhere north of Dallas. Mr. Laird was a wealthy man and I think they named a hospital after him over there.

Like many, Joyce is saddened to hear of the closing of his old home course in Palestine. He said the best round of golf he can remember was a 63 one day at Palestine's Meadowbrook in a money game where "they gave me the gimme putts of about a foot or less." He remembers many rounds with his friend and business partner Leroy Roquemore, who won the Meadowbrook Invitational in 1953, beating future British Amateur champion Joe Conrad along the way.

Joyce added:

> There was some pretty good golf played there. Of course Leroy played it every day before he went over to Tyler to play. We used to go to the different towns and play matches with people. We would go to Nacogdoches and Jacksonville and Tyler... I tried to invest a little in the oil business. Leroy and I accumulated a few minerals around. We had a little interest in the oil business.

These days, Joyce spends his time at home in Palestine or with his daughter at her home near Colorado Springs. He has been playing more tennis than golf but concerned about his balance on the courts. He said he fell a couple of times and would have to be sure to find a grass or clay court if he wanted to play again.

How about playing golf again?

"I'm threatening to," he said.

Consider yourself warned if you happen to draw him in whatever flight. He may not be too talkative.

More Center

"There is no place in the world like Center, Texas."

Eddie Lyons

Shreveport, Louisiana

Eddie Lyons has always been a fine golfer. A whiz kid on the links in his hometown of Shreveport, he won the Louisiana State junior championship and looked forward to a professional career in golf like most young players. But Lyons never reached the PGA Tour like two other guys who grew up in his hometown–Hal Sutton and David Toms.

But Lyons never lost his competitive desire and at the still-young age of 29, found himself on the verge of winning a mighty big amateur tournament at the little course in Center. Needing only two putts from about 15 feet to win, Lyons lagged up very close to the cup. Instead of marking his ball and waiting, he wasted little time in tapping in for the championship in 1981. He had defeated such good players as Oklahoma State regulars Willie Wood and Andy Dillard, who finished second and third, one and two strokes behind Lyons.

Lyons described it:

Man, my feet never stopped moving until I putted out. I remembered a similar situation several years earlier when Billy Pierot had a one-shot lead and lagged a beautiful putt up next to the hole from the very front of the green. He then politely waited for everyone to putt out and then froze over his putt and missed it. I mean it was only 10 inches but the pressure got him and I wasn't going to mark my ball and go through the same agony. Pierot went into a playoff that year he missed the putt and lost to Lindy Miller.

When Lyons won in 1981, the tournament was reaching its pinnacle in terms of quality of field and size of the Calcutta. The field was probably as good as or better than big-time amateur events like the Trans-Miss or the Southern. It certainly began to have fields better than the state amateur and that wasn't too popular with some. "I heard that's what got the tournament in trouble," Wood said. "That year in 1982, the Center tournament was up against the state amateur and most of the really good players elected to play at Center."

That was in 1982 when the Texas state amateur was contested just up the road at Crown Colony in Lufkin. It was won by Scott Verplank with John Slaughter of Abilene finishing second. So the state am was not devoid of talent that year. It is just that players like Dillard and Billy Ray Brown and Danny Briggs were in Center and not at the state am. But who could really blame them because Center was not only a great tournament with great competition. Center was FUN. There was beer and good barbecue and pretty girls, just for starters.

In 1980, Center really put on a show for the players with Miss Texas, Lex Ann Haughey, appearing as the special guest at the women's fashion show on Saturday afternoon and then staying to watch the conclusion of the tournament on Sunday. She may have stayed longer than anticipated because a five-hole playoff ensued between Oklahoma State's Bob Tway and little known Carl Baker of nearby Nacogdoches. It was Baker who prevailed in an upset and received the trophy, a kiss from Miss Texas, and maybe a little cut of his buyer's winnings in the Calcutta.

It was the second straight year to lose in a playoff for Tway, the tall and fluid swinger who won the 1986 PGA Championship at Inverness in Toledo, Ohio, by holing out from a bunker just off the 18th green in the final round. Tway pulled the rug out from under Greg Norman that day and won seven other times on the PGA Tour but in 1979 at Center he again lost on the fifth hole of sudden death, this time to OSU teammate Kevin Harrison. The win by Harrison delighted a syndicate of women who bought him in the Calcutta because "he is cute and we can afford him."

Harrison wasn't the first guy that the ladies bought with their scientific method. Three years earlier, handsome Joey Hager of Dallas won the tournament and thrilled the women's syndicate.

"Joey bought me a nice dinner that night just because I was riding back to Dallas with him," Lamar Haynes of Dallas said. "The ladies even told me the reason they bought Hager was because they thought he was nice looking."

Hager and Haynes were teammates at SMU for one year in 1976. A senior that year, Hager played the tour for a year or two but did not achieve much success. He did have one top 10 finish in the U.S. Open at Pebble Beach in 1982 and thus played in The Masters the following year.

Another Dallas pro, Dean Overturf, had a solid amateur career that included a win at Center in 1971. He was a little before Kite and Crenshaw at Texas but never did too much on the PGA Tour. He did qualify for a few senior tour events with his top finish a second place to Hubert Green in Mexico in 2000 and the largest check of his career—$110,000.

The era of playing for big money in the Calcutta at Center was essentially the late 1960s through the 1970s. Most who participated in the Calcutta adhered to what became known as the *law of the west*. That was the unwritten law that the buyer who won gave the player about 10 percent of the winnings. Some players bought part of themselves which meant possibly winning more money but definitely more pressure.

Exhibit one of the *law of the west* gone awry involved Bob Rawlins of Dallas. Known far and wide as *Dark Cloud* because of his negative but clever sense of humor, Rawlins made only one trip to deep East Texas.

"I went down there one year and tried to buy part of myself but the guy who bought me said, 'don't worry about a thing, we'll take care of you,'" Rawlins said. "Well I finish third behind Mike Mitchell and Hal Underwood and ain't seen a dime yet."

The pressure on some was intense because of the large amounts of money involved in the Calcutta. One player was in contention with nine holes to play and because he owned part of himself, was in position to make a lot of dough. He hit from the elevated tee on the first hole, his 46th of the 54-hole competition, and just killed the drive. Hitting a high hook on the downhill, dogleg left, he was only about 50 yards from the green, if that far.

"I got to thinking about all of that money and I couldn't catch my breath," he said. "I had this little half wedge to the green and I was having trouble breathing."

A lot of the young golfers from that era can attest to a different kind of pressure than playing for junior or college trophies. "It's very different," one player said. "The young kids today who play the junior tours have no idea of what it's like to play in a Calcutta tournament where there is money involved. That brings about a different kind of choking and really prepares you for the pressure of playing professionally."

After the NCAA and USGA cracked down on Center in 1982, the tournament continued as an open event to pros and amateurs. The winners were less famous names but fine players. And one was even a bit of a character and had the audacity to challenge the *law of the west*. This player came to the 18th at Center with a commanding lead of some four or five shots. He lagged his first putt up to within about three feet of the hole and called for a ruling. Joe Pro, the alias for the club pro at Center, was called out of the gallery for a ruling about what? Joe Pro said:

> He called me out and said you need to go tell so and so that if he doesn't cut me in for a lot more than ten percent, I may just slap this ball off the green into that pond and make things interesting. So I go over to his buyer and tell him what the deal is and his buyer tells me to go back and tell him that "we don't play it that way in Center, Texas, and to go ahead and hit the ball into the lake and we will just see what happens after that."

After hearing back from Joe Pro, the talented young player with such bravado meekly tapped in his par putt and thus obeyed the *law of the west*. He lived to play again, still welcome on the late, great beer and barbecue circuit.

* Longtime Center Country Club member, Billy Bob Thomason, passed away in August of 2011. "He was the bestest friend I ever had." Center Golf Pro - Joe Whittlesey (Joe Pro)

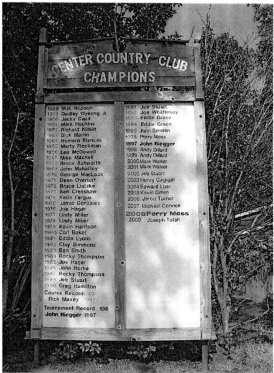

The list of winners near the putting green at
Center Country Club

Trigger

Watching him on the final nine holes the year he tied David Price at Briarwood (1972) was really something.

Don Robert Johnson

Tyler, Texas

They sat beneath the towering pines together on a warm and delightful summer evening in East Texas. One was a veteran of the beer and barbecue circuit and the other a rising national star of amateur golf soon to turn pro. There was a mutual respect as players of the game, but even more of their love and knowledge of it.

The two men marveled at the spectacle being played out in front of them at this tiny course tucked away in the sticks. The auctioneer bellowed out in rapid cadence the accomplishments of the particular player being sold to an eager and mildly intoxicated crowd of poultry farmers and others who wanted to be a part of the fun.

It was Calcutta night at Center in 1973. Sitting under the pines and enjoying conversation were and A.J. Triggs of Tyler and Ben Crenshaw of Austin. For Crenshaw, only 21 years old and turning pro just a few weeks later, it was a second trip to the *best little golf tournament in Texas* and a chance to redeem himself after a less than pleasing performance the previous year. It was also a chance for *Gentle Ben* to soak in the atmosphere one last time of a Texas tradition that goes back to the 1930s–the local beer and barbecue tournament. For Triggs, it was a swan song for an amateur career of many years. He had chosen to sell life insurance rather than fight to eke out a living on the pro tour. And now, at age 43, Triggs was fighting against time to remain competitive in the Championship Flight.

Triggs said:

I remember us sitting there and watching that Calcutta. They had those pick-up trucks backed up in there under the pine trees and enough barbecue chicken to feed an army. It was Crenshaw's last amateur tournament. They sold me and Mark (his son) as a team and of course Ben later went for a bundle.

Crenshaw was indeed the high seller that night and came through three days later by famously holing a 10 or 15 foot side hill putt on the final green down by the pond. Such is the stuff of legends. But when you speak of beer and barbecue legends, perhaps none is bigger than Triggs.

For starters, he was painfully short off the tee. His best tee shots traveled only 225 or 230 yards in the persimmon era. But Triggs was known for accuracy as he rarely played from outside the fairway. And then there was his unshakable course management. He knew his capabilities and his limitations and usually hit the proper shot accordingly.

Longtime friend Don Robert Johson said:

Watching him on the final nine holes the year he tied David Price at Briarwood (1972) was really something. He hit the green on the 13th hole that was very tight with traps on both sides of the green and I asked him if he hit a seven-iron. He said, "no, Bucket, that was a five-iron and I got all of it." The hole was only about 140 but he was tired from the heat and felt like that's what he had to hit.

Later in a playoff with Price, Triggs conceded a short putt to Price on the third hole of sudden death. Johnson rode back to the clubhouse with Triggs on his cart and questioned him about giving a two-foot putt.

"He told me that Price was going to make it anyway but that he also didn't want to have to decide whether to lay up or try to carry the water on the next hole. He always hit driver there because it was about a 200-yard carry," Johnson said with a laugh. "He was just amazing to watch in those days."

Triggs played in 21 straight Briarwood Invitationals from 1958 through 1978. He thought, and rightfully so, that it was one of the top amateur events anywhere in Texas. "I thought it emerged with the top college fields in those days," Triggs said. "It was probably the best of all of those tournaments because it was a good course. I also liked the tournament at Pinecrest in Longview a lot."

One year at Pinecrest, Triggs prevented Jacky Cupit from winning the tournament for a third year in a row. They were tied going into the last hole when Cupit, playing in front of him, looked to make birdie but had hit a ball into the water and actually made par. This was pointed out to Triggs by his father who was riding with him that day. Knowing that, Triggs was able to get up and down from just short and right of the green to win. "It was a difficult putt on some grainy greens but it went in," Triggs said. "It was a big win for me but disappointing to all of the Longview people who wanted Jacky to win. He was a great player."

Triggs won the first Briarwood tournament in 1959 but later Cupit proved just how good a player he had become when he won the Briarwood tournament in 1960. Briarwood was still played on the original nine holes but it is amazing that Cupit never made a score higher than a four on any hole in the 54-hole event.

What made Triggs such a good player for so many years, in addition to his accuracy and course management, was a consistently superb short game. He was an especially efficient chipper, using a variety of clubs as the situation might dictate. Those familiar with his chipping and pitching would wage even money on him getting up and down from 50 yards and in. That was a safe bet.

During a spring four-ball barbecue tournament at Tyler's Briarwood one spring, Sale Omohundro played with Triggs and went home to Sherman impressed:

I had heard from my dad that Mr. Triggs was really good around the greens... Then we played together and he was getting up and down when he needed to but I didn't think much of it. He was playing with Mark and they had a decent round going and then Mr. Triggs chips in on the last two holes. I mean they went in like putts.

It was after the second straight chip-in that Omohundro let out a scream that could be heard several holes away. "ARE YOU KIDDING ME!"

Considering the tiny greens at most East Texas courses, the chipping prowess of Triggs paid huge dividends in the barbecue tournaments. Looking back at the statistics, usually a few under par won the tournaments that generally were 54-hole medal play during the 1960s and 1970s. But Triggs also excelled in match play and won two Willow Brook Invitationals at his home course in Tyler during the 1950s.

"He beat some really good players at the Willow Brook tournament," T.C. Hamilton, who grew up at the Tyler course, said. "I caddied for him the year that he beat the Mexican Amateur champion to win and I know Phil Rodgers was in the field one of the years that he won."

Unlike his college teammates at the University of North Texas like Billy Maxwell and Don January, Triggs never touched a golf club until after he finished high school in Dallas. He was a good high jumper in high school and became interested in golf through his friend Buster Reed, a really good amateur golfer for years on the barbecue circuit and a college roommate. Soon Triggs was breaking 80 and not long after that shooting par or better.

His first beer and barbecue tournament was the summer after his freshman year in 1948 when he traveled to Kilgore for the Meadowbrook Invitational. It was a memorable event in many ways. Triggs said it was so hot that summer that several of his practice balls melted in the shag bag and "I just poured them out on the ground." Then there was the crooning of Don Cherry in the parking lot after the Calcutta when grown men and women became teary eyed listening to a masterful version of the Bing Crosby hit song, the Irish lullaby, *Tura Lura Lura*. And finally, he witnessed a classic match between his friend Reed and the king of the circuit in those days, Earl Stewart, Jr. Reed prevailed but it was considered an upset.

Triggs said:

The only match that I heard was better was when Earl and Gene Towry went sudden death in a tournament in Ranger. I think they birdied every hole for about seven holes and even tied a hole with eagles. Towry finally won and it was typical of Gene because he was as tough a competitor as we ever had at North Texas.

At his first tournament at Kilgore, Triggs was in the third flight and ran into some tough competition. The conventional wisdom of those days was to play in the first or second flight but don't mess up and get into the third flight. The wisdom was borne of experience because the third flight was usually the preferred flight of proven *sand baggers*. These were men who could play but knew the only way to win was to inflate their handicaps and not have to play against the *flat bellies*, aka college boys.

Triggs added:

I ended up beating Skinny Garrison in the finals. I won a suit bag and thought I was on top of the world. I really wasn't a very good player then but I was learning fast and getting to play with such good players as I got to play with at North Texas certainly sped up my improvement.

Triggs' college career was interrupted by a stint in the Coast Guard and when he returned, he was the co-captain of a 1954 team that played well but lost the NCAA to an SMU team that featured the Addington brothers, Don and Floyd. Triggs then moved to Tyler in 1955 and began his career in sales.

Joining Willow Brook Country Club, Triggs won many club championships and also an invitational hosted by the club for many years during the late 1940s and 1950s. The tournament eventually gave way to the Briarwood Invitational across town but featured great fields. One of the Willow Brook members, Paul Price, acted as the catalyst for the tournament by traveling to college tournaments and recruiting the best players, much like Joe Bob Thomason did for years at Center.

Triggs won the Willow Brook event twice while another member of Willow Brook, Leon Taylor won it during its early years in the late 1940s. Taylor was an institution at Willow Brook with his legendary air travels in his *Texas Bullet* and the money games he played with partner Raleigh Selby of nearby Overton.

Triggs said:

My best Leon Taylor story concerns a couple of my North Texas teammates. Billy Maxwell and Buster Reed actually hitchhiked from Denton to Kilgore to "fleece us some old men." Well Billy and Buster learned a hard lesson that day because Leon and Raleigh took them for every dime they had on those little sloping greens at Kilgore. They were both begging lunch money for about a month when they got back to school.

Another fine player during the late 1950s at Willow Brook was left-handed Jack Wilkerson. A deft wedge player himself, Wilkerson was a perennial winner of the state left handed championship played every year in Seguin. He recently passed away and Triggs and another good player at Willow Brook during those years, Chad Hanna, paid their respects to the Wilkerson family. It was also a chance to recall a classic match between Triggs and Wilkerson for the club championship. The two men halved eight straight holes in sudden death with Triggs finally winning the par-five ninth hole with the car lights shining on the green near the Willow Brook clubhouse.

In 1964, Triggs began a long association with the Texas Golf Association by acting as tournament chairman for the Texas Amateur held at Willow Brook and won by Marty Fleckman. Since that involvement, he has served for more than 35 years with the TGA with two terms as president. He has acted as the starter for the Texas Amateur for almost 40 years and said the 2012 tournament at Lakewood Country Club may be his last in that capacity.

Having grown up in the Lakewood area and attending Woodrow Wilson High School, starting off the top amateurs at the historic Dallas course that is celebrating its 100th year will be a like coming full circle for Triggs. He has played a lot of good golf and been privileged to see even more through the years. Fortunate for many who love the game, he is graced with a vivid memory so that he can share it when given the opportunity.

That thought brings us back to the night of chatting with Crenshaw under the pines at Center. It was just a couple of legends visiting about a game they both love.

Not East Texas

"Once you get west of the Trinity River, you're not in East Texas anymore."

Bill Holcombe

Corsicana, Texas

It is a story that tells a bigger story.

A longtime member is telling of his recent trip to play some of the best courses in Northern California. He had the great privilege to play Cypress Point, the Alistair McKenzie designed jewel on the Monterrey Peninsula that is ultra-private.

"We finish playing and I go into their tiny pro shop to buy some souvenirs," the member said. "And there is an old guy in there and he said it is cash only or charge it to your club. And I said, 'Sure, I am a member of Corsicana Country Club.' And this guy is old and he said, 'We've had some people from your club come through here before but let me see if you are still in our book.'"

"After a little while, he comes back and says, 'Yeah, you're still in our book. Charge the whole darn pro shop if you want to.'"

The member smiled.

"That is one of the most fabled courses in the country along with Augusta National and they knew us here in little old Corsicana. It made me feel good."

When the member, Paul Hable, returned to Corsicana, there was one small item of business that needed to be handled. "I called our secretary here and told her that when an envelope hit the club from Cypress Point in California to immediately call me at work. I wanted to be sure a check went out that day to pay our bill. I'd hate to anyway mess up our standing out there."

The larger story is about how a little country club in Texas became so well known at one of the most prestigious courses in California. It is the story about how one guy who loved golf hit it big in the oil business and thus could afford to share his love of the game to the benefit of many in a small town 50 miles south of Dallas. It is the story of H.R. "Bill" Stroube. Stroube is the man most responsible for why Corsicana Country Club is one of only six Texas courses designed by the esteemed A.W. Tillinghast.

Orphaned at age 9 due to the untimely death of both of his parents, Stroube and his younger brother W.C. "Corny" Stroube hit a couple of big oil wells just outside of Corsicana in 1924 and parlayed that initial success into a long and prosperous family business. Soon after the two wells in Corsicana, the Stroube brothers, partners until death, began buying leases and royalties in the East Texas field that came in shortly afterwards and wheeled and dealed with folks like H.L. Hunt, probably the most famous of the Texas oil barons of that time.

But it gets even better. Stoube's love for golf led him to not only join the new and highly reputed Brook Hollow Golf Club, another of Tillinghast's Texas designs, but also to travel west to California to play some golf with others in the oil business such as Howard Hughes. The subject of much attention because of his flamboyance and extraordinary wealth, Hughes was originally from Shreveport and got the golf bug for a while during his heyday of making movies in Hollywood. He worked hard on his game but after receiving a lesson from Dallas golf pro Ralph Guldahl, the winner of two U.S. Opens, he quit the game. During the lesson, Hughes supposedly asked Guldahl if he could become good enough to win the U.S. Amateur. When he received a negative answer from the pro, Hughes never touched another club.

"Granddaddy and Howard Hughes were good friends and once Hughes sent his own doctor to look after one of my uncles who had been kicked by a horse," Frank Stroube of Dallas said. "And he never sent my grandfather a bill for any of the services."

A strong and athletic man, Bill Stroube loved golf and played well. He made sure that Tillinghast was involved in the building of a second nine holes in Corsicana. He knew that a course designed by the same man who did Brook Hollow and Winged Foot in New York would be challenging. Stroube also played the best courses in California as often as he could.

"I remember my dad telling me that he went with Bill and Corny and another guy in two cars from Corsicana to California," Glenn Taylor of Tyler said. "They started off playing Los Angeles Country Club and then Bel Air and then made their way up the coast to Cypress Point."

Taylor's father Leon was an oilman during this time and a fine golfer. Stroube also played well and was a member of the clubs they played. There is a picture of them, along with Stroube's son Jack, on one of the tee boxes at Cypress Point. So Corsicana Country Club's good standing with Cypress Point goes back to the late 1940s.

"My grandfather and his brother were two men who made a lot of money and knew how to enjoy it," Frank Stroube said. "When I was a kid living in Abilene, every summer I would take the train to Santa Monica for a month's vacation."

The Stroube brothers are not the only Corsicana Country Club members to enjoy some golf at Cypress Point. Another member, Don Marett, joined the club in 1963 when he moved from Fort Worth to Corsicana.

Marett was a fine amateur in his day, winning the club championship at Ridglea Country Club in Fort Worth numerous times before doing the same at Corsicana. He hailed from Georgia and met his wife while attending Auburn University in Alabama. His son Rod, who lives in Austin, said his father's most famous golf match was against Sam Snead.

"My dad doesn't like to talk about himself but I have heard the story and he doesn't deny it that he once beat Sam Snead in a money game in Boca Raton, Florida," the younger Marett said. "My uncle Abe Dietch of Pittsburgh was a wealthy man and a member of the Boca Raton Club for years and set up the match. Sam didn't like getting beat by an amateur and showed it with his behavior."

Back in Texas, Marett partnered with Tommy Parnell of Ridglea to win the inaugural Champions Cup at Champions Golf Club in Houston in 1961. Because of that win, Marett was invited to play in the 1962 Bing Crosby and partnered with Chi Chi Rodriguez.

Marett said:

My wife and I stayed with Mary Sargent and just had a ball. It was very cold and actually snowed that year. Chi Chi only brought silk clothes from the Caribbean and almost froze to death. But we had a great time with my wife dancing with her Hollywood favorite, Ray Milland, one night.

Mary Sargent was a fine woman amateur in the 1950s and lived along the famously beautiful 17-mile drive near Pebble Beach and Carmel. Trying to find her house, Marett asked a gardener nearby for directions and was told that the Sargent house was just down the road next to the ice plant.

"I drove all over looking for an ice plant," Marett said with a big grin.

Like a lot of first-time visitors to California, Marett did not realize that ice plant is a devilish vegetation that looks pretty but wreaks havoc for a golfer who might find a ball resting in it.

Marret still has a scrap book put together by his late wife that is definitely a trip down memory lane for those who are baby boomers or older. Just a quick sampling of the celebrities who played in 1962 and some with their handicaps: Fred McMurray; Tennessee Ernie Ford (12); Bob Hope (11); James Garner and Phil Harris. Don Cherry and Tommy Bolt were paired together that year as were Doug Ford and Texas amateur Dudley Wysong.

Corsicana Country Club was awarded the Texas State Amateur tournament in 1951. It was won by Joe Conrad of San Antonio. Still match play in those years, Conrad defeated Fred Moseley on the first hole of a sudden death playoff after they played the 36-hole finals match to a draw. It was a bitter pill for Moseley who played in the 1949 and 1950 Masters. The year before at Oak Hills in San Antonio, Moseley lost to Austin's Morris Williams, 5-4.

"I just remember him storming out of there," Conrad said.

In those days, Corsicana Country Club hosted an invitational that many say was the equivalent of Center. Former Corsicana pro Max Stewart showed me a copy of a column written by former golf writer Harry Gage of the Dallas *Morning News* that talked about the tournament in 1951 and all of the Dallas golfers who would be playing like Jack Munger, Spec Goldman and Earl Stewart, Jr.

Stewart had defeated Munger in the finals the year before. Munger, called *Mungo*, was a colorful player who helped bring the U.S. Open to Northwood Club in Dallas in 1952. It was a new club at that time and Munger felt the publicity of the U.S. Open would help sell memberships. That tournament was won by Julius Boros who also won the 1963 U.S. Open at The Country Club in Massachusetts and the PGA Championship at Pecan Valley in San Antonio. Boros is still the oldest man, at age 48, to win one of golf's majors.

Munger is legendary as far away as Cherry Hills Golf Club in Denver where he once holed a chip shot from the patio area of the clubhouse over the 18th green. He won that club's member guest, The Hillsdilly, in 1953, with his Cherry Hills partner John Bell.

An exerpt from Gage's column in 1951 reads like this:

Texas golfers will point their cars towards Corsicana this week and the thirteenth annual Corsicana Country Club Invitational, which begins Wednesday and runs through Sunday.

Earl Stewart, Jr. of Dallas and Longview is expected to be on hand to defend the title he won last year by defeating Jack Munger of Dallas, 2 and 1.

Paul Bruce, general chairman of the tournament committee, said indications are that this year's classic will be even larger than the 1947 affair which attracted 160 players. Stewart, incidentally, shot a 59 for the medal prize last year.

Esteemed as one of the state's most colorful and enjoyable tournaments, the Corsicana Invitational this week should be the greatest ever held. Bruce and his committee have laid plans for a gala occasion.

A stag dinner will launch festivities Wednesday night after the qualifying play. Visiting ladies will be honored at a luncheon Thursday by the Corsicana Women's Golf Association, after which a cocktail party for the players and the ladies will be held at 5 pm. The informal dinner dance will be staged Saturday night as the concluding social event.

Dallas will be well represented with Munger, Bud McKinney, Herbert Durham, Clarence Kloppe, Jr, Arthur Corbin and Reynolds Smith heading the list from Big D. The Dallas Country Seniors at DAC may keep several others away.

Six flights of thirty-two each are planned with the low 192 qualifying. The finals for the title will go thirty-six holes while the finals for all other flights set for eighteen holes.

The winner of the 1951 Corsicana Country Club Invitational was local golfer Gilbert Stubbs, who defeated Goldman in the finals.

SECTION II: WEST TEXAS

"It's just insane out there."

Chris Hudson
Tyler, Texas

Above: On the course reporters for the televised Odessa Pro-Am
Below: Gallery at the Odessa Pro-Am, circa early 1960s
Please note the corporate sponsor

From Quanah to Ozona

"Do they have flights in the State Amateur now?"

Ben Hogan

Fort Worth, Texas

There is just something about West Texas. The desolate beauty of wide open spaces and the flat terrain that stretches forever into the horizon can play tricks with the mind…as can the hot dry weather and a constant wind that blows tumbleweeds along a barren ground dotted with scrawny mesquite trees. Then there's the elevation out on the plateau. Does that affect one's thinking, one's attitude? There is definitely something mystical about West Texas. Whatever the cause, the folks who play golf out on the plains seem to have one thing in common–they want to have fun with a capital F.

"Did you see that closed circuit TV screen in the 19th hole?" a young Dick Crawford asked his partner, dapper Doug Sanders, in the locker room at Odessa Country Club during its famous pro-am in the early 1960s.

"Naw. What about it?" Sanders said.

"Someone stuck a wedge in it! There ain't no picture on it now," Crawford said.

The two-time NCAA champion from the University of Houston and his flamboyant pro partner doubled over in laughter as they headed for the parking lot and a quick exit. They were headed downtown to the party at the Lincoln Hotel, also known as the Golden Rooster.

Crawford had just holed a shot for an eagle on the 18th hole to salvage a so-so round and more importantly extricate Sanders from some heavy bets. Whoever they got even with must have taken out his displeasure on the TV set.

"I have a theory about West Texas," an East Texas golf pro who played college golf at Texas Tech said. "They are shut in a lot of the winter and they drink heavily until springtime. Then they get out into the thin air and heat and their brains are just fried. It's insane out there."

Obviously spoken in jest but how else could one explain the stories that emanate from the high plains where every little town west of Fort Worth seems to have a golf course and an invitational tournament. Those tournaments usually involve some golfing, some drinking, and a little bit of gambling.

Bigger-than-life John Paul Cain, the 1961 Texas state amateur champion said:

> *I guess my favorite tournament was a deal they called The Tournament of Champions that they had out in El Paso. It was at the Ascarate Park golf course and sponsored by the El Fenix Mexican restaurants. It was for all of the guys who had won barbecue tournaments that year. Well, they had five temporary greens so all of the guys are whining and moaning. Since I can't putt, I am thinking this is mighty fine. They are giving away Mido watches for the low round each day and a Rolex for the tournament winner.*

Cain, an archetypical West Texan known as the *Sweet Swatter from Sweetwater* continued:

> *I was low three of the four rounds and won the tournament. So I went home with three Midos and a Rolex. I traded one of the Midos for a case of whiskey and gave the others away as Christmas presents—one to my barber and one to the one-armed guy who cleaned up at night for my dad's bank.*

Dan Jenkins couldn't make up a story better than that. They still make Mido watches in Switzerland that now sell for $500 and up.

Cain, a winner of two Champions Tour events, was even the butt of a joke from none other than Ben Hogan one day in Dallas. "Hogan and Byron Nelson were waiting to play an exhibition match and they announced me as the state amateur champion from Sweetwater and I commenced to top my drive about 40 yards," Cain said. "Then I hear Hogan say pretty loudly, 'do they have flights in the state amateur now.'"

Who said the *Wee Ice Man* from Fort Worth had no sense of humor?

Cain can keep a listener spellbound for hours with his stories of the beer and barbecue circuit in West Texas. And one quickly surmises that his antics are the rule rather than the exception.

Set in West Texas, some might say that the movie *Tin Cup* was a little outlandish with Kevin Costner hitting ball after ball into a lake to blow the U.S. Open on the last day. No one felt too sorry for him since he ended up with the girl, Renee Russo. But that movie was dull compared to the stories of the plumber from Lubbock, Roland Adams, a real life *Tin Cup*.

"After a pro-am one time at Lubbock Country Club, a lot of the guys ended up drinking down the road at the Elm Grove golf course," retired golf professional Jack North said:

> Roland makes the statement that he can hit a one-iron off the sidewalk over the clubhouse, which is two stories high. I said, "partner, you can't hit a one-iron over that clubhouse," and he said, "you go get me a darn one-iron." I had one in my trunk. By now it's two in the morning and everyone is drunker than hell. There's no telling how much money is piled up against him hitting this one-iron over the clubhouse. We pull the cars up with the lights shining on the clubhouse. He throws a ball down on the concrete and opens the clubface like he was going to hit a bunker shot and hits a little high cut over that clubhouse. As he is gathering up all of the money, he says, "y'all want to try this again?" And everyone says, "yes, you're drunk and you can't do it again." He drops another ball on the sidewalk and does it again. Then I look at my one-iron and there is just a tiny scratch on the bottom of it—amazing! I think he made about $800 that night.

But is he really a plumber?

"Yes, he just worked on my house a week ago," North said. "He is such a great guy that he won't take money from me for the work so I have to give it to his wife."

Sometimes Adams would not even change into golf clothes but head to the course in his plumber's gear.

"A friend of mine calls me from another golf course in town and says there are two guys here who want to gamble," North said. "It was a Monday morning. And he said, 'can you play?' And I said, 'yeah, I can probably get away but how good are they?' And he said they look pretty good warming up. They can hit it."

"I said I'll go get Roland. So I go and pull Roland out of a ditch. I mean he has got four-buckle overshoes on, bib overalls and an old shirt and an old air conditioning hat on sideways. And I said, 'hey I got a pretty good gamble for us.' And he said, 'well I can come back and do this later.'"

"He had been up all night drinking and working and we go to Elm Grove. He makes seven pars and 11 birdies and did not putt real well. Every shot was right next to the hole. He shoots 60 on that track and is drunk, hung over and in four-buckle overshoes."

Roland Adams, now in his 70s and plagued with a bad knee and hand, is said to have won more than a hundred beer and barbecue tournaments in West Texas. "He never wanted any limelight or notoriety," North said. "He would win and then get his Calcutta money and go home. He didn't even want the trophy. He was the best player that I have ever seen."

Robert McKinney is another former Texas state amateur champion and a golf purist. He quickly corroborates North's testimony. "I can't disagree with that statement," McKinney said. "Anything Jack North tells you about Roland Adams is absolutely true. I think some of that *Tin Cup* stuff must have been taken from stories about Roland."

McKinney, a Houston architect who is a member of Champions and a former Texas Tech golfer, played the West Texas circuit for years with three friends that still get together each year to play golf and talk about the good times. They call themselves the four musketeers and completing the group are John Shepperson of San Angelo, Jess Claiborne of Lamesa, and Steve Thompson of Odessa.

"Through the years we played in a bunch of the barbecue tournaments and still like to talk about them," Shepperson, who now lives in the Dallas suburb of Allen said. "Our wives think we're crazy but we love our golf."

The four musketeers played in the barbecue tournaments during the late 1960s and early 1970s. Like the others who played the West Texas circuit, the expanse of small towns that had nine-hole courses and an invitational, though mind boggling, did not deter their travel plans.

On any given weekend in West Texas there might be a tournament in Pampa and one in Ozona, some 350 miles away as the crow flies from the north to the south. Or consider simultaneous events in Wichita Falls and Andrews, just 250 miles apart on an east to west grid.

Shepperson said:

> We would all pile in a car when we were in high school and go play in a tournament somewhere. We would load up and go to Fort Stockton or Lamesa or Andrews or McCamey or some of those other West Texas towns like Ozona and Big Lake and play some golf. You could find a golf tournament somewhere out there in West Texas almost every weekend. I won a couple in Ozona and Sonora and one in Fort Stockton. Then there was Tahoka and Idalou. Heck, Idalou might have had a tournament every other week.

Learning the game as caddies at their respective home courses, the four musketeers all became good amateurs and all but Claiborne played college golf at Texas Tech. Claiborne played at TCU in Fort Worth.

"We all grew up in West Texas," Thompson said. "Robert, Jess and I, and Shep, we all grew up within two hours of each other. I know that sounds like a long way off but in West Texas that wasn't very far. We played the junior circuit as kids and became friends to this day. We make it a habit of getting together a lot."

The four musketeers agreed that the Top of Texas Invitational in Pampa was one of the best of the barbecue tournaments. Thompson said:

> It was always Labor Day and you didn't know what to take because it could a hundred degrees or a cold front would come blasting through and it would be freezing. But it was just good people up there. I stayed with friends there and they treated you like a king. Even though it was an individual tournament, guys wore their college colors. Everybody who was a good amateur was playing in Pampa.

Another former Texas amateur champion who played the West Texas circuit was Bill Holstead of Wichita Falls. He played in a lot of them but had a special affinity for the ones in Quanah and Vernon.

Holstead added:

> Quanah is one of those nine-hole tracks with tees, greens and dirt. There wasn't a blade of grass out there on the fairways or the rough. I'm out driving these guys 50 yards every hole but scooping and sculling my wedge off that hard pan. Finally I was watching Jack Williams of Plainview warming up there one time and he could really play. He was practicing his 100-yard six-iron shots and later told me that you have to have that shot to play the hard pan.

Holstead won his share of barbecue tournaments but has a fond memory of getting beat one year in Vernon. "Dave Eichleberger and I are in the last group and it is really slow going the last day on that nine hole course," Holstead said. "He is up on me a few shots with nine holes to go and there is about a two-hour delay before we can tee off for the last nine. I go into the clubhouse and the craps game is still going so I jump in. When they called us to the tee, I am up $1,600. Eichleberger wins the tournament but I drive home as the leading money winner."

Despite the high jinks, there was some serious golf played on the West Texas circuit and some great players developed their skills. One of the biggest events each year was the Men's West Texas Amateur first played in 1925. It is believed to be the third oldest tournament in Texas with only the Texas State Amateur started in 1906 and the Texas Open first played in 1922 being older.

The tournament is rotated to a different course each year and has been won three times by four different players. Holstead won in 1967, 1978, and 1979; Williams in 1953, 1957, and 1963; Tom Doughtie of Amarillo in 1989, 1990, and 2006; and Morris Norton in 1936-37 and 1940. McKinney won it twice in 1969-70 as did such well known West Texas golfers as Don Cherry in 1951-52, Bobby French in 1949-50, John Farquhar in 1971-72, and Jeff Mitchell in 1975-76.

One-time winners of the West Texas amateur that went on to have successful careers on the PGA Tour were Billy Maxwell in 1948, Ernie Vossler in 1954, Charles Coody in 1959, and Bob Estes in 1987. The tournament is now played annually as the West Texas Amateur and has been run by the Texas Golf Association since 2003.

McKinney said:

Texas is a very big golfing community. The Texas Golf Association didn't come to West Texas very much so there was a West Texas Golf Association that also took in Eastern New Mexico. I played in the Men's West Texas starting in high school and all through my college years. It's kind of a sad story in a way because I played in it during its zenith when players from all over the state were coming in to play. It gradually degraded to a point where it was like a handicapped club event or something... When the Texas Golf Association took it over, it began to come back in it's stature. It's still not quite back to what it once was. In the early days, it was very close in stature to the state amateur.

The Greatest Tournament in the World

"It was absolutely the greatest tournament in the world."

Bill Holstead

Wichita Falls, Texas

Ben Crenshaw once described the Masters as a celebration of golf that comes around each April. It could be said that for 20 years, from 1949 until 1969, the Odessa Pro-Am was a celebration of West Texas golf.

Holstead is not reticent in his description of the four-day event that traditionally was held in July opposite the British Open. "It was absolutely the greatest tournament in the world, no doubt about it."

The brainchild of Odessa Country Club golf professional Shorty Hornbuckle (hard to make up a name that good) and several other prominent businessmen, the tournament started as just a chance for club pros to bring their top amateur and play in a scratch event on a fine West Texas golf course. It later grew to involve touring pros and celebrities such as Dean Martin, who played several years with Cherry.

Some of the top touring pros through the years made it to Odessa. Among those playing during the 20-year run were Pro Golf Hall of Fame members Byron Nelson, Jimmy Demaret, Cary Middlecoff, E.J. "Dutch" Harrison, Tommy Bolt, Raymond Floyd, and Lee Trevino. Trevino played in 1966, the year before he finished fifth in his first U.S. Open and two years before he won that tournament and became famous.

Mickey Jones is an attorney in Odessa and a board member of the Texas Golf Association. He learned a lot about competitive golf as a youngster caddying in the Odessa Pro-Am and he enjoyed rubbing elbows

with the game's top players and the celebrities who played.

"We are kind of isolated way out here so we create our own entertainment," Jones said. "I think that helps explain the popularity of golf in West Texas. Watching those great players up close was a learning experience that I have never forgotten. You learn how the good players think and manage their games. The tournament was fortunate to have some major championship winners come and play each year."

In addition to the top touring pros, the Odessa Pro-Am also showcased the best college golfers of that time.

The Arkansas Traveler, Dutch Harrison, left, watches perhaps the greatest amateur of all time, Charlie Coe, at the Odessa Pro-Am, circa early 1960s

"There were two amateurs who carried their pro to the winners' circle," longtime Odessa Country Club member Ronald Crain said. "The first one was Marty Fleckman in 1963 and then a few years later Grier Jones out of Oklahoma State."

Crain personifies the West Texas mentality–tell it like it is. "One year Raymond Floyd was in the locker room complaining that no one was out watching him play," Crain said. "I asked him what he shot and he said 66. So I told him that if he played a little better, he might get a bigger gallery."

Fleckman was one of the top amateurs in the country during his college days at the University of Houston in the mid 1960s and though a product of Southeast Texas, always played well in Odessa:

It was in 1964 and I was playing with a pro from Port Arthur, Ned Johnson. I was playing unbelievable golf. I was making six or seven birdies a round. And Ned was hanging in there. So we are tied going into the last hole with E.J. "Dutch" Harrison and George Archer, who was his amateur partner. I hit a good drive and hit a wedge to about three feet. I made the putt and we won the tournament. Right after that, George Archer turned pro.

Archer would go on to win the Masters in 1969 and for years was considered the best putter on the pro tour. Fleckman admired the level of play in the pro-am:

Man they had some great teams out there. That was one heck of a tournament. In 1966, I played with Babe Hiskey and we either won it or finished second. For some reason, I always played well out there. They had a big Calcutta and some pari-mutuel betting. I remember Bobby French used to play with Bo Wininger and Byron Nelson played in it one year. There were just a lot of good players.

French, a successful Midland oilman now retired, helped Hornbuckle promote the tournament. He always played with Wininger, a talented pro who enjoyed the high life. From Commerce, Oklahoma and the same high school as Mickey Mantle, Wininger died prematurely of a heart attack in 1967, at age 42. He played the tour before purses amounted to anything and had moved to Las Vegas to represent one of the large hotels just prior to his death.

More than just a tournament, the Odessa Pro-Am was quite a party. "There has been a number of occasions when people had to leave the tournament pretty much incognito for a variety of reasons–winning bets, welching on bets, you name it," McKinney said. "But it was all in good fun."

Cherry, now 88 and living in Vegas with his wife Francine, enjoyed his time playing with Martin in Odessa. "I was a little worried the first year we played," Cherry said. "I asked Shorty what if we don't make the cut? He said, 'Don't worry, whatever you and Dean shoot is going to be the cut.'"

Martin, the host of a popular variety show on TV that Cherry frequently appeared on as a guest, did wonders for the attendance. During the years that Martin and Cherry played in the mid 1960s, the tournament usually had crowds estimated at 7,500 or more.

Don and Rik Massengale of Jacksboro were both successful amateur and professional golfers. Don played his college golf at TCU during the late 1950s with good friend Coody while Rik was a star for the University of Texas in the late 1960s. They teamed up to win the 1966 Odessa Pro-Am. Don, who won twice on the PGA tour, died in 2007.

Rik, a three-time winner on the tour, remembers playing in the festive tournament said:

The first year I played in it, Don and John Farquhar were defending champions so Don got me a partner. It was Ray Floyd and he was young and incredibly good. We finished second and he didn't give me a dime and I thought he might... later I gave him a hard time about that when I got out on the tour.

Don Cherry and Dean Martin played in it and Don and I played with them the year that we won. It was kind of a zoo with the gallery. It was my first experience with a gallery not interested in golf. They were out for the party. Neither Don nor I were ever much for the parties. We just went out and played and then back to our room for some rest.

Another crowd pleaser for years was Harrison, dubbed *The Arkansas Traveler* since he hailed from Conway, Arkansas. A member of the PGA Golf Professionals Hall of Fame, Harrison is still an underrated player who turned pro at the age of 20 in 1930 and won 18 times on the PGA Tour. He won both the Texas Open and Bing Crosby Pro-Am in 1939 and finished tied for third in the famous 1960 U.S. Open at Cherry Hills behind Arnold Palmer and Jack Nicklaus. Harrison even qualified for his last U.S. Open in 1971 at the age of 61.

Also well liked by his fellow pros, Harrison was known for his sly tricks when it came to club selection. Homero Blancas played as his amateur partner in the early 1960s. Blancas said:

I played with Dutch Harrison and it was so funny because just about every hole he would say, "I want you to do this" We were playing a money game before the tournament started and he said I want you hit this five-iron and leave it short. So I just busted it and it came up short and he says out loud, "I'm gonna hit three-iron." And he would hit it on the green and say, "I hit that good." Then the other guys would hit it over the green and make bogey, so we made some money that way. Dutch could really finesse those iron shots. He would feather it. It was a money game and he teaching me the hustle. He said they may be better than us but we have some tricks up our sleeve.

Tour players of Harrison's era, and even of Blancas', did not make the big checks as they do now. In fact, one of the best players to ever come out of West Texas, Billy Maxwell of Abilene, made his biggest professional check the last year of the Odessa Pro-Am in 1969. Since the amateurs could not split the money, Maxwell took home the entire winners' check of $8,000. That amount was greater than any check he made with any of his seven PGA Tour wins.

"When I say that all of the great players came from West Texas, I am speaking of Billy Maxwell, and guys like that," Cherry said. "Of course the only time Billy ever beat me was at the Fourth of July Invitational in his hometown and he beat me on the 37th hole. I still haven't gotten over that."

Cherry did mention that he managed to beat Maxwell on 10 other occasions. He wouldn't be much of a Texan, especially a West Texan, if he hadn't mentioned that.

Billy Maxwell receives winning trophy from
Odessa Pro-Am founder Shorty Hornbuckle

Rik, left, and Don Massengale enjoy a soft drink after the
final round of the 1977 Bob Hope Classic won by Rik

From Sand Greens to the Tour

"We grew up pumping gas and fixing flats."

Rik Massengale

Dallas, Texas

On Camp Bowie Boulevard in Fort Worth is an endearing and enduring symbol of what lies to the west. It is a giant jackalope perched atop a billboard. Some jackrabbits get so big in West Texas that they grow antlers and morph into jackalopes. Or so the legend goes.

Nevertheless, one highway leaving Fort Worth goes to Jacksboro and jackrabbits still race across the landscape along the way. From the small town of Jacksboro, some 60 miles west of Fort Worth, came two superb golfers, brothers Don and Rik Massengale. The Massengale boys grew up playing the sand greens on Jacksboro's nine-hole golf course and went on to win important amateur tournaments and forge successful careers on the PGA Tour.

Don, who was 10 years older than Rik, died in January of 2007 and left a void in the lives of friends and family. One of those close friends is Charles Coody, a fellow West Texan who grew up in Stamford and now owns the Diamondback Golf Club in Abilene. Both men spent quite a bit of time in Fort Worth during the late 1950s as teammates on the TCU golf team.

Rik lost his older brother who was both his close friend and mentor while Coody lost his lifetime friend from their days traveling together two summers on the West Texas barbecue circuit. Don began having some heart problems at a tournament in Florida several years before his death. His heart beat began to speed up dangerously but he was prescribed medication that seemed to remedy that malady. So when he died suddenly of a heart attack, it was quite a shock to family and friends.

"He was 10 years older than me but we were real close," Rik said. "His death was real tough because it took us all by surprise. He had been given a clean bill of health by his cardiologist but then shortly afterwards had the heart attack that killed him."

Don turned pro in 1960 and won two tournaments on tour in 1966, the Crosby and the Canadian Open. He lost the 1967 PGA Championship in an 18-hole playoff to fellow Texan Don January.

Joining the Champions Tour in 1987, Don won twice. During his time between the tours, he took a club pro job in the Conroe area and won the 1972 PGA Club Professional championship which may have somewhat assuaged his disappointing loss to January. His two sons, Donny and Mark, are still teaching golf professionals in that area.

Don won the Odessa Pro-Am twice as a pro, once with amateur John Farquhar of Amarillo and once with his little brother when Rik was still an amateur. Rik said he was like his older brother in that they did not go in for a lot of the partying and gambling like a lot of the others players at the Odessa Pro-Am. They liked to play and then go back to hotel and rest.

Part of that demeanor may have been influenced by their upbringing in a small West Texas town and their association with Henry Richards. Richards was a successful businessman in Jacksboro who loved golf and liked to help young players who had bright futures in the game.

"You would have to look a long time to meet a nicer man than Henry," Coody said. "He liked to help young players by taking them to tournaments or getting them some good equipment. He was a good player and even sometimes helped them with their swings. He helped a lot of kids from Jacksboro, not just Don and Rik."

Despite being a fellow West Texan, Coody said he first met Don at TCU when he went there on a golf scholarship in the late 1950s. He roomed with Don the first year before moving to a fraternity house for the rest of his stay in college. After the two men graduated, Don was excused from military duty because of bad knees and turned pro while Coody spent three years in the service before doing the same. With Coody still an amateur, the two played together in several Odessa Pro-Ams.

Coody said:

What's funny about that is that Don and I had a deal that we would split everything 50-50. If you finished in the top five, the pro got the winnings and the amateur got a watch. Someone had already bought another amateur's watch before I got mine and *when they presented it, Don yelled out that we had another watch for sale. Well someone gave me $100 or something for it real quick. What Don was doing was making sure he got his half of that watch, which was funny, but it was only right.*

At Don's funeral, Coody recounted the early years of their friendship:

I talked about us meeting at TCU and how we played together in college. Then I talked about how we traveled together all one summer on the barbecue circuit. That started with the state amateur in San Antonio and we split the gas money the rest of the summer. We probably played in 12 or 13 tournaments that summer.

That was the summer of 1959 and Coody won the state amateur at Oak Hills over Dudley Wysong of McKinney. Don was the defending champion that year since he won the title at San Angelo Country Club the year before.

Don's close call at the PGA was a tough loss that Coody was familiar with through his own disappointment at the Masters in 1969 when he faltered at the end to lose to George Archer. While Coody rebounded to win the green jacket in 1971, Don never captured a coveted major.

"It's always tough when you have a chance to win a major and don't for whatever reason," Coody said. "He had a 71 to January's 69 during the playoff so it was only a couple of shots difference and not like he made a double bogey on the last hole or something like that."

While Rik never won the state amateur championship, he finished as the runner-up to Hal Underwood at River Plantation Golf Club in Conroe in 1968 but won the prestigious Cotton States Amateur in Monroe, Louisiana in 1967 and the Western Amateur in 1968. Rik turned pro in 1970 and claimed three wins on tour at Tallahassee, Hartford, and the Bob Hope Classic.

Rik said:

I guess I had sort of an advantage growing up because I got to tag along with Don to the tournaments and play with him in Fort Worth. I got to meet all of his buddies like Gay Brewer, Charles Coody, Jack Montgomery, Rex Baxter and a bunch of those guys. So the Odessa Pro-Am was not as big a deal as it might have been for someone who had not been around the pros as much. But it was a very special time because we played so well that week.

Rik said their father owned a gas station in Jacksboro that sold tires. "We both grew up pumping gas and fixing flats," Rik said. "But we got that done in the morning so that we were playing golf in the afternoons. It wasn't really hard work."

According to Rik, Richards was their unofficial golf coach and way ahead of his time in helping young golfers. "He would go to the pro tournaments and film their swings and then show you the different positions. It was very primitive but it was the only film we had ever seen of golfers."

Rik now sells real estate in Frisco, a North Dallas suburb, but fondly remembers his early days of golf with Don in Jacksboro:

> *We had sand greens until my senior year in high school which would have been 1965. The flag was always in the dead center of the green so you would step off how far you were from the hole and then you would smooth this trail with an iron that had a piece of pipe on the end. You got to where you could lean on one side of the pipe and make it break one way or the other. You would ease up on the drag near the hole so that you could hit it as hard as you want and not worry about it going past the hole.*

From such a beginning, the Massengale brothers started a golfing journey that would lead them to such venues as Augusta National and Turnberry in Scotland. It is a journey that Rik now cherishes more than ever.

A Kentucky Gentleman in West Texas

"Sorry about the misidentification but you have the check."

Bobby Jones

Atlanta, Georgia

He is a handsome and mild mannered man whose golf game and professional record have largely gone unnoticed for many years. He survived a near fatal car accident when only 16 and much like one of his heroes, Ben Hogan, overcame it to achieve much success on the course.

Not a native Texan, this Kentucky gentleman received a football scholarship to Texas A&M from arguably the most famous college coach of all time and then never played a down. He was kidded by the great Hogan and once received a humorous letter from Bobby Jones that he still displays in his home in Naples, Florida.

Bobby Nichols of Louisville, Kentucky learned to play golf well in College Station and then based out of Midland when he first turned pro. He went on to win 11 times on the PGA Tour with one major, the PGA Championship at Columbus (Ohio) Country Club in 1965.

His name is always coming up and did so again when Jack Nicklaus was asked his memories of playing in Houston just before he set out for an exhibition match with Arnold Palmer and Gary Player at the Insperity Championship. Nicklaus said:

> *I remember the 1962 Houston Open at Memorial Park like it was yesterday. I had a two-shot lead and my caddie could not get the pin out of the hole on a birdie putt late in the last round. So he pulled out the entire cup and my ball hit it dead center. I went from*

a two to a five and tied with Bobby Nichols and Dan Sikes. Nichols won the next day in a playoff.

Nichols connection to the beer and barbecue circuit came from his years of playing out of the Midland Country Club, just down the road from Odessa and the Odessa Pro-Am. He played in it many times, first as an amateur and then as a pro.

Nichols said:

I played in it a couple or three years with Boyd Huff, who was the Midland Country Club golf professional. And then I played mostly with members of Midland Country Club. It was kind of a fun event. I played in it at least five years. We had a fun time because Don January and Billy Maxwell and Doug Higgins had sponsors from that area. Jimmy Demaret and Byron Nelson played in it and George Archer played in it a few years.

We had a lot of really good players in it. (Cary) Middlecoff played in it and so did Mike Souchak. Mike always played with Eddie Chiles, who owned the Western Company. I actually worked for his company for a while. Eddie would always bring Souchak and that was the way it was. Al Balding played in it and (Dow) Finsterwald and Doug Sanders played in it. A lot of the guys were brought out there by guys who had money and wanted to sponsor players and have a good time. They had a nice Calcutta.

Nichols said a lot of the early PGA Tour events also had a Calcutta. "I can recall in 1960, of the 18 events, 15 of them had purses of 15 grand or less. And that's the total purse. So it wasn't a whole lot of money and so they would compensate with a Calcutta and sometimes you made more money that way than with the official money."

As a pro, Nichols played in the Odessa Pro-Am with members of his adopted Midland Country Club:

We had a bunch of fun. I played with a friend named Sleepy Wynn who was a member of Midland Country Club. We played a couple of those years with Jimmy Demaret and he always had Don Cherry. And Cherry was a very good amateur back in those days, in the 1950s but obviously his singing was his number one thing. But he was a very good golfer. We got along real well. It was just a lot of fun with a lot of laughter. During the tournament there was always casino night with a lot of gambling and the Calcutta and it was a week-long party.

Nichols made his way to Texas after a high school career in golf that was necessitated by the horrible car crash that was a result of a high speed joy ride. He was paralyzed for a couple of weeks from the waist down but regained the use of his legs through physical therapy. He also overcame a horrible concussion. The injuries made it imperative that he not play contact sports but his football coach before his injury had a good connection for college.

My coach played for Bear Bryant. I got hurt in a car accident my senior year and my high school coach asked him if they would consider giving me a scholarship. And this was in 1954, my senior year, when he (Bryant) was going to Texas A&M. I couldn't play anymore so I started playing golf. One thing led to another and Coach Bryant said come on and we will give him a scholarship.

He (Bryant) was also the athletic director so he was running the whole show. In those days the scholarships were unlimited. They had 103 players on scholarship but when they got back from Junction and 10 days, only 32 came back.

The Junction he refers to is the subject of a book by Jim Dent about how Bryant whipped his Aggie team into shape with a brutal off campus training camp in the middle of nowhere, Junction. As a result of the severity of that training camp, NCAA rules now forbid any training off campus. Gene Stallings and Jack Pardee, both famous football players and coaches, survived that camp.

Bryant later mellowed and built a dynasty at Alabama that still remains one of the greatest accomplishments as far as total number of wins and national championships. But the man in the hounds tooth hat also had a real soft spot in his heart for Nichols and showed it every year at Augusta during the Masters.

In the early 1970s, Coach Bryant would come over every year. My birthday is April 14th so it would fall during the tournament sometimes. A couple of years running, under the big tree in back of the clubhouse, he had a table set up with a birthday cake that said, "Happy Birthday Bobby." Guys would come around and have a bite of cake and so forth. He would stand around there and talk with everyone. I was really surprised that first year but that's the kind of guy he was. It was pretty special.

Nichols, who won the Southwest Conference championship during his sophomore year at A&M, played in The Masters 17 years running. He finished second to Gay Brewer in 1967 and got to visit with Jones at one of the cottages near the 10th tee. Jones was in a wheelchair at that point.

Nichols won the 1964 PGA to really jumpstart his career. It was played in Columbus, Ohio and Jack Nicklaus tied for second with Arnold Palmer. Not a bad duo to beat early in his career but Nichols remembers another detail about his final round that later led to some kidding from one of the game's legends. "I played with Mr. Hogan the final round," Nichols said. "It was kind of ironic because I had played with him when I was in Midland. When the pro at Midland Country Club would go to Fort Worth, we would always play with Hogan." He continued:

> Later that year, I played with him at the World Open (the first tour purse of $200,000) at Oakland Hills in Michigan. We played together again the final round and I won again. So after the tournament, as I am checking out of the Radisson Hotel in Birmingham, Michigan, the next morning, when I walked down the stairs and went over to the check-out counter, Mr. Hogan was checking out. So I was back behind him waiting and when he finished, he turned and saw me and said, "You ought to pay me to play with you."

"All I could say was, 'Mr. Hogan, anything you want, sir. I'd love for you to.'"

Hogan later sent Nichols a telegram congratulating him.

Perhaps Nichols' favorite story, though, occurred in 1970 when he won the first $300,000 purse at the Dow Jones. He took home the winner's check of $60,000. A couple of days later, he received a letter.

"I opened the letter and there is an article from the Charlotte paper. It had my picture on the bottom of the page and said that Bobby Jones wins the Dow Jones," Nichols said. "Along with it was this letter."

> Dear Bobby,
>
> Congratulations on the win. Sorry about the misidentification but you have the check.
>
> Best of luck always,
>
> Bobby Jones

"I still have the letter and it is dated 1970. He passed away in 1971. I have the letter in my house and it's framed. I was totally surprised because he took the initiative to write such a nice note and send it to me."

Like Jones, Nichols is a thoughtful gentleman and like Hogan, a man who overcame adversity to forge a memorable career in golf. He still plays as often as he can and recently partnered with Homero Blancas at the Liberty Mutual Legends of Golf in Savannah, Georgia.

A Texas Sized Story

"I was just over there with no one to defend me and that got me interested in the rules."

Joe Black

Austin, Texas

Joe Black is a big man. He is Texas big at 6-foot three and 200 pounds. Like a true Texan, Joe Black has a big story to tell. It is a story of rags to riches; of rising from obscurity to the public limelight and from utter insignificance to a prevailing authority. It is the American Dream personified.

After years of sharing stories from his career at the top of the PGA of America and the PGA Tour, Black was persistently encouraged to write those stories down for the golfing world to enjoy. At age 77, Black accepted the challenge and penned a book that uses small vignettes to capture his big story. An enjoyable read, *A Few Good Golf Stories*, is a collection of 72 stories, brief but entertaining. The tidy number is symbolic of an official competition or even par round.

Long known as a pre-eminent rules expert, Black takes the reader behind the scenes with tales that range from barely escaping Cuba before Fidel Castro invaded Havana to penalizing Jack Nicklaus for slow play. The stories keep the reader engaged as Black reveals that he consulted with Lord Derby and others to change the Ryder Cup competition and once had to give marching orders to former president and supreme allied commander Dwight D. Eisenhower. Only in golf are such things conceivable for a boy who grew up poor in West Texas.

Black's story begins in deep and remote West Texas. A small town on Highway 87 between Lubbock and Big Spring, Lamesa is far removed from tree country. It is flat and dusty and the winds blow constantly. One of six children in a three-room house without indoor plumbing, Black shared a bed with his brothers on the back porch in this small farming community. This was in the late 1930s, tough economic times in America.

But Lamesa had a nine-hole golf course and a club pro whose last name would later be synonymous with the game. Shanty Hogan ran every aspect of Lamesa Country Club and gave Black his start in the golf business. At first he worked on the course, watering the greens and tees, but soon he moved into the golf shop. The main benefit was getting to play regularly and thus develop a good golf game. It was a golf game that allowed Black to compete at the top level of junior tournaments. The generosity of others helped with expenses.

It was at a high school tournament at Odessa Country Club that Black first became interested in the rules of the game. He experienced an aberration when a Midland golfer did not finish a hole but was still awarded a trip to state because of a consensus decision by the coaches to "give" him a putt that he did not hole out. "I was just over there by myself and had no one to help me or defend me and that got me interested in the rules," Black said.

After earning a scholarship to Hardin Simmons and playing on a national small college championship team, Black turned pro and later worked for a stint at Ross Rogers Golf Course in Amarillo. He enjoyed working there but jumped at a chance to go to work for the PGA Tour in 1958.

At his first tournament, the Los Angeles Open at Rancho Park, Black made 36 rulings during the opening round. It was a thorough baptism as a rules official. "They had a driving range in the middle of the course and all kinds of screwy stuff," Black said. "And we are doing this out of our car because they didn't have golf carts then. It really motivated me to learn the rules. They are a big part of running a tournament."

Black soon became the tournament supervisor for the tour as it was rapidly gaining popularity through the advent of television. Arnold Palmer had star power that was enhanced by the arrival of Jack Nicklaus and Gary Player, who were marketed as the *Big Three* of golf.

Known for a calm demeanor that was epitomized by his ever present black framed eye glasses, coat, and tie, Black dispensed rulings on tour and at the Masters that were never challenged.

Black said:

I never got excited. I would take the time to open the rule book and show it to the player. So I wasn't making the ruling, the book was.

My theme was always let the rule book make the ruling. You don't need to get into a confrontation with a player. The only time you have confrontation is in slow play and things like that.

Enter Nicklaus at the Portland Open, circa 1962.

"I think he was testing me to see what he could get away with in regards to slow play," Black said. "Once I determined that he was not making an effort to speed up, I assessed him a two-stroke penalty before he signed his card. Later we discussed ways that he could play faster."

To his credit, Nicklaus accepted the penalty without an argument and went on to win the tournament. This was at the start of a playing career that most golf historians rate as the best ever. Nicklaus even alluded to the penalty later as helping him become a better player.

Black was involved with Nicklaus in another discussion years later that resulted in the current Ryder Cup competition that is so popular today. At the 1977 matches at Lytham and St. Annes in England, Black and an American contingent led by the president of the PGA of America, with Nicklaus as its player spokesman, lobbied the British PGA and its royal representative Lord Derby to change from a British and Ireland team to a European team. The British later agreed and the 1979 matches featured the first European team with Seve Ballesteros as its young gun. The rest is history.

The encounter with Eisenhower took place in Palm Springs in 1964. The final round of the Bob Hope was played at Ike's home course, El Dorado Country Club, and finished with a tie between Jimmy Demaret and Tommy Jacobs. Ike wanted to follow the match in his golf cart but there were no gallery ropes in those days and Black felt it could cause a disruption of play. He therefore told the former president that he preferred that he not follow the match. A gentleman and true lover of the game and its competition at the highest level, Ike gladly complied and said he would watch on TV.

While Eisenhower was still president, in 1958, Black came close to an unwanted encounter with Castro during social upheaval that led to a change of power in Cuba. The tour was playing an event in Havana and told to be careful. Two weeks later, Castro entered the city and violently seized control of the government.

Black said:

The event was uneventful except for one incident involving Julius Boros, George Bayer, and Bill Collins. Their cab was stopped by the military. A machine gun was poked in the window and they were told to get out of the car. The cab was searched for weapons they thought the guys might be smuggling into the city. These three men were three of the biggest guys on tour but they were meek as lambs during this incident.

Associating with former presidents and avoiding future dictators is a long way from watering the greens at Lamesa Country Club.

Arnold Palmer, often described as the *King of Golf*, described Black's book best. "I know that it will bring many memories to all who have followed the game and enlighten those who weren't around at the time.

Joe Black during beer and barbeque days

Bones

"On the tee, the winner of 10 PGA Tour and 22 Champions Tour events, the winner of the PGA Championship, his nickname is Bones, Mr. Don January."

Announcer at the Insperity Championship

Houston, Texas

His tall and angular form was easily recognizable on the PGA Tour during the 1960s and 1970s. With a slow and easy gait and the back collar of his shirt turned up to block the sun, he was the epitome of cool before anyone knew about Rickie Fowler. His demeanor made Jason Dufner seem the nervous and chatty type.

There is a lot more to Don January than hitting a golf ball. The native son of Dallas learned to play at Stevens Park and went on to become a star on the PGA and Champions Tour. But more than that, he was an active advocate for the betterment of professional golfers. In his own vernacular, he was a doer and not a watcher. "My wife used to ask me why I had to be on so many committees," January said. "And I just told her, 'Honey, somebody has got to do it.'"

The two most significant changes in professional tour golf brought about during January's involvement as a player representative were the repeal of the repugnant "Caucasian only" rule in 1962 and the separation of the tour from the PGA of America in 1968.

In 1962, Charlie Sifford became the first black golfer to play the PGA Tour and later won an event in Hartford, Connecticut. Lee Elder became the first black professional to play in the Masters in 1975 and the Ryder Cup that same year. Before Sifford's acceptance by the PGA, black players could occasionally get into tournaments up north or in California but lacked full membership. Sifford suffered many indignities during those years of segregation. He said he only wanted to prove that he and other black players belonged in the tournaments strictly on merit–they were good enough to compete and win.

"It was the right thing to do," January said. "Even an idiot would know that the rule was unfair. But it took some doing because we had to change the constitution of the PGA and that meant each section has to approve at the annual convention that October."

January's involvement with that change was through his participation in the Tournament Bureau of the PGA of America. This was in 1961 before the split of the tour from the PGA of America. On that committee were four players and four members of the PGA of America. At that time, to play the tour, a golfer had to be a member of the PGA of America and that was not possible from 1934 until 1961 if the golfer was not Caucasian. To remove some of the shame from that rule, the PGA of American awarded membership posthumously to several outstanding black professional golfers from that era: Ted Rhodes, Bill Spiller, and John Shippen.

About five years later, the tournament players sought out January to go back on the Tournament Bureau to work with the PGA of America for a split. The players would separate from the PGA and form what is now the PGA Tour. January did his part and helped orchestrate a smooth transition but he and a few others suffered some bad publicity because of it. The players were called greedy by some in the media but hindsight says January and his peers were right in their efforts.

That January was a champion for fairness to all golfers is not surprising. Growing up in the Oak Cliff area of Dallas as the son of a roofing contractor, January was taught the meaning of work and the value of a dollar. He didn't play the beer and barbecue circuit consistently while in college because he was expected to help with the roofing business during the summer. But he did manage to play in some tournaments and won a few as might be expected.

In his college days most of the barbecue tournaments were match play and January said he learned that such a format wasn't his forte. "I wasn't worth a darn at match play," he said. "I would get up on a guy and just relax or something. I did much better in medal play where it is more about playing the golf course."

His golf began as a young boy who would wade in the creeks of Stevens Park while golf pro Wiley Moore let him keep his shoes and clubs behind the counter in the pro shop. Later he would play with the balls he had found. As he became older and more accomplished, he would play at Lakewood Country Club on weekends. His dad, A.C., joined Lakewood and January would ride the city transit to the course from Oak Cliff. His initial golf, however, was at Stevens on a $10 annual membership bought by his dad.

The January golfing clan in those days included A.C., A.C., Jr., who went by Ace, and Don. "The A.C.," January said, "was for Alaric Cradoc."

"My grandmother saw the name in a book and just liked it," January said. "I remember attending my brother's high school graduation at Fair Park and when they called out Alaric Cradoc January, I heard someone in the back say 'there sure are a lot of foreigners going to school these days.'"

The January clan was anything but foreign as they hailed from Central Texas. It was upon his return from a visit to relatives in Central Texas that January realized his boyhood friends could now outhit him on the golf course and he didn't like that. So he stood all of one evening on an elevated tee and hit balls until he could clear a creek below.

"I guess that's where I got this long old swing that has served me well," January said. "I don't care who you are, you want to be able to knock the hell out of that ball. You just have to learn to control it, too."

After a good college record at the University of North Texas (North Texas State in those days), January did a stint in the service before turning pro. He played in some barbecue tournaments, especially in West Texas, since his wife to be, Pat, was living there at that time. After 56 years of marriage, January's wife passed away a couple of years ago.

January explained:

We met at North Texas because she was in a golf class that I was teaching to pay for my college in those days when they couldn't give golf scholarships. The girls like to take golf because they didn't have to take PE and get all sweaty. She had on a pretty blouse and I didn't have a chance. I called it entrapment but she is the one who had to put up with me all of those years.

One interesting thing about January's wife's family was that they knew Ben Hogan's parents in West Texas. Hogan's mother worked for a while for January's father-in-law before moving young Ben and his brother Royal to Fort Worth after the untimely death of Ben's father.

"I never knew about that until Ben had already retired," January said. "It's funny that my wife's family knew the golfer I most admired. Hogan was very good to me when I went back on tour in the mid 1970s and needed some new equipment. He could not have been better to me than he was."

It was just after his college days that January played as an amateur with Dallas pro Harry Todd to win the 1951 Odessa Pro-Am, a fun-filled event played in by the likes of Byron Nelson, Cary Middlecoff, and Tommy

Bolt. Later, in 1960, January was the pro on the winning team with amateur Dick Jennings of Lubbock.

January won his first tournament on the PGA Tour at the 1956 Dallas Open played at Preston Hollow Country Club. He holed a bunker shot for an eagle on the final hole to win. Preston Hollow has been closed for a long time but was located near the intersection of Hillcrest and Forest Lane in North Dallas. He went on to win 10 times on the tour but it was after some time off, around 1976, that January played his best golf.

January said:

> *I got off of the tour to do some golf course development but the economy shut that down. So I told my wife that I would go out for a year and see how I can do. That was in 1975 and we had three kids in college. I won the Texas Open that fall and then had my best year ever in 1976. I won the Vardon Trophy that year* (lowest scoring average for the entire year). *My last round was at Pensacola and my caddie said to me, "Well, you did it." And I said what did I do and he said I needed to shoot 71 or better to win the Vardon Trophy and I shot a 68. I am just glad I didn't know beforehand or I probably would have shot 75 or something.*

Of his initial win in Dallas, January fondly recalled being more nervous than he had ever been or has been since. He said he had just three putted the 17th hole to go one behind Dow Finsterwald and Doug Ford. He said the last hole was a dogleg right down a hill with some trees forcing the drive to be hit high.

"I hook the ball so I really had to hit it over those trees," January said. "But I got down there and the ball was in the bunker. I wasn't a great sand player and hit this shot that hit about three feet up the pole and just fell in. Then I had to sweat Finsterwald and Ford but neither birdied."

His longtime friend and teammate at North Texas, A.J. Triggs of Tyler, was greenside when January holed the winning shot.

"I remember it like it was yesterday," Triggs said. "I saw him coming out of the scorer's tent and he was shaky like a leaf. But it was pretty special for him to win that way and to get his first one in his hometown."

With that he was off and running on a career that lasted for 35 years with his dominance in the early 1980s on the newly formed senior tour. He amassed 22 wins on the senior circuit but perhaps even more noteworthy is that he was involved in the formation of that tour and won the first tournament played.

As he said, he's a doer.

Abilene's Masters Champion

"He noticed it and went over and examined my clubs real closely. And I just went, 'oh boy.'"

Charles Coody

Abilene, Texas

The shot is still vivid in his mind after more than 60 years. At his first ever professional golf tournament, the 13-year-old boy was simply amazed.

It was the 1950 Colonial National Invitational Tournament and tiny Jerry Barber had hit his second shot long on the par-4 second. To Barber's dismay, the ball lay in the middle of a wide and deep tire track in the soft soil over the green. He called for a ruling but was told to "just play it" from an official who never got any closer than about 30 yards away. It was obvious even to a young boy that the official did not like Barber.

The young boy watching could not believe it when Barber calmly straddled the rut with his back to the hole and with one hand chopped down on the ball. The ball popped up and hit the ground running as the over spin propelled it first up the hill and then down. The ball rolled to within six inches of the hole for a tap-in par.

"And I thought, 'Boy, these guys are good.' And that was long before the PGA Tour came out with its slogan. There wasn't a blade of grass on that hill behind the green in those days."

Having seen the great Ben Hogan hit practice balls the day before, the teenager was still pondering what he had seen at Colonial when he went back to West Texas with his uncle. At dinner that night, he told his mother and father he enjoyed the golf and now knew what he wanted to do when he grew up–play professional golf.

The young boy was Charles Coody of Stamford and his career plan turned out to be a good one. After an amateur career that included a Texas state amateur championship in 1959 and qualifying for the 1960 U.S. Open, he indeed became a professional golfer and enjoyed many good years on tour, highlighted by winning the 1971 Masters.

But his mother wasn't so sure about his golf plans and Coody had to make her a promise. "From that point until I finished college," Coody said. "My mother was always afraid I would quit school to play golf. I promised her that I would finish college before playing professional golf."

It was during college at TCU that Coody developed his game to a level capable of playing the tour. In addition to the state am title in 1959, Coody also spent an entire summer traveling the barbecue circuit with teammate Don Massengale. The following year, in 1960, Coody won a barbecue tournament in Tyler that helped him pay his way to Denver and Cherry Hills for what many still call the greatest U.S. Open ever played.

Playing golf at TCU was not a given for Coody when he left high school. Instead, it was a love of basketball that steered him to Fort Worth. "I was a Longhorn," Coody said. "The night I graduated from high school, I was going to Texas. I was about 95% sure. I wanted to play basketball and Texas said I could but wasn't excited about it. Then TCU began to recruit me more for basketball and that's why I went there. Later, I found out that those two sports don't mix."

While at TCU, Coody became better acquainted with Hogan. He would watch Hogan hit his own practice balls sometimes at Rivercrest Country Club. Coody had no idea that he would later play Hogan equipment and even incur the mild wrath of the stoic man. Even more memorable was a round he would play with Hogan years later at Champions Golf Club in Houston.

Coody said:

When I first turned professional, I was in the Air Force and living in Fort Worth. That was in 1963. The Hogan Golf Company at that time just had Ben as the only one with an agreement to play the equipment. Of course it had his name on it. They decided to sign a couple of pros to play their equipment in the summer of 1963 and that was me and Frank Wharton of Dallas.

With his new equipment contract, Coody began a new phase of his longtime relationship with Hogan. "I had the opportunity to play with him a couple of times at that time before I went out on tour," Coody said. "If I hadn't been a little intimidated by him and asserted myself more, I could have played a lot with him… I didn't and I regret that."

Coody said Hogan did not play the tour too much then but he was paired with him three or four times that year:

I always enjoyed it. I loved watching him play—the preciseness of when he struck the ball. It had a different sound because he hit it solid... The only problem he had, and I witnessed this, because he used to come out to Rivercrest and practice while I was at TCU, was when his knees were bothering him. His leg action was just unbelievable, that's what created so much of his distance.

But when his legs were bothering him, it had an effect on his shots. Coody said he saw, from a distance, the problems that his bad legs caused.

I remember this one particular time he came out to practice and was having some problems with his knees. He was well into the shag bag before he began to hit the ball decently. He was hitting balls fat and so forth and when you do that, it's a sign that your foundation is not right, which is your legs.

Filing that memory away, Coody pursued his own career and liked the Hogan clubs but not the ball. He knew it was inferior to the Titleist ball. He also liked a Spalding one-iron that Ridglea Country Club pro Raymond Gafford had given him in college and used a driver made by another manufacturer in Memphis. These minor deviations ultimately caused a conflict with Hogan. "I played with Hogan at Colonial in 1966 and I teed off with it (the driver) on the 7th hole, which was different then and he noticed it and went over and examined my clubs real closely," Coody said. "And I just went, 'oh boy.'"

Anyway, I got a call from the guy, the GM of the company, the next Monday morning. I lived in Fort Worth, and he said can you come out, I need to talk to you about something and I knew what it was about. He said, "Ben noticed that you were not using all Hogan equipment and he wants to know why." I said that the one-iron is a club that I have had since college and I haven't found anything that I like as well and the driver is just that I have not been able to find a shaft for my Hogan driver. And he said, "If we make them for you, will you play them?" I said of course I would. But he didn't make them and I got a letter that fall terminating our agreement. Which was fine, I wasn't living up to the contract, which I understood.

Coody said he hated to part ways with Hogan but was happy to finally play a better ball. He said it might have been a coincidence, but he finished third at Houston in his first tournament playing new irons and a new ball.

Having won the Dallas Open in 1964, Coody did not win again until the summer of 1969 at a tournament in Cleveland. He was making a good living on tour, however, and came close to winning the 1969 Masters won by George Archer. He remembers being so close to winning when he thought himself out of a six-iron and hit a five-iron into the back bunker at the par-three 16th at Augusta to doom his chances in 1969.

As fate would have it, he faced the same situation two years later when at the top of the leader board on Sunday. This time, he went with the six-iron and knocked the ball stiff to birdie and go on to claim the green jacket. It was a win to mark a great career in golf and each year he gets to relive it to some degree by attending the champions' dinner.

Just about a month after his Masters win, Coody also had fate pair him one last time with Hogan. It was the tour event at Champions Club in Houston and Hogan was persuaded to play by his good friend Jimmy Demaret, who founded and ran the golf club with Jackie Burke, Jr.

Another in attendance for Hogan's last round at Champions was a veteran of the beer and barbecue circuit, Bill Runte of Houston. "I will never forget the first hole," Runte said. "Hogan drives into a fairway trap and then tops it out with a four wood. He just cold topped it."

It didn't take long for Coody to notice the gimpy legs of Hogan and begin to dread the inevitable:

He was like one over through three holes and the 4th hole was a par-three. It was a two-iron back then. The first tee shot he hits is fat and goes down into the barranca. Then he re-tees and hits his 2nd ball fat without considering a possibility of going up there for a drop. Then hits a third ball that hits up but bounces down into the barranca... So we go down there to see if his ball has carried any part of the barranca and he climbs down into it, which he shouldn't have done with bad knees.

At this point, Coody said that he and playing partner Dick Lotz of California are cringing for the great man. Hogan finally finishes the fourth hole with a 9 or 10 but continues to play. Hogan made a couple more bogeys but had steadied somewhat when he reached the shorter but just as treacherous par-three 12th.

The green runs along the pond and the bank is cut short so that anything that hits on that bank will roll down into the water. And again he hits the ball a little fat and it hits and rolls down the bank into the water. I am looking at him and it is so odd because he reached down and grabbed his tee and stood up and his eyes just went straight to mine and he said, "I am sorry, I just can't go." And he handed me the card that he was keeping. I was stunned a little bit but not badly. I felt the agony that he was going through. He was a very prideful man and he was having a horrible time. It was all physical—his legs were just not working.

Coody becomes silent for a moment as he reflects on the memory. "And so he walked off the tee and there was a golf cart waiting so I thought maybe someone from the club was following him. The tour was much looser then and he just got into the cart and the caddy got on the back with his clubs and they rode off. Into the sunset I guess you could say... But I never thought about that being his last competitive round."

Times are different now for Coody but he still enjoys hitting balls and playing at the course he owns in Abilene. He designed Diamondback Golf Club and it is a little bit of Augusta in West Texas. It is a fun and challenging course that golfers of all skill levels seem to enjoy. The course gets especially busy in the fall when the hunting season cranks up in West Texas and outdoor enthusiasts can shoot doves in the morning and shoot for birdies in the afternoon.

Coody still competes occasionally. He looks forward to playing in the Liberty Mutual Insurance Legends of Golf each year in Savannah, Georgia. It is a reunion of sorts when he plays in the Demaret Division for players 70 and older. In 2012, he partnered with Dale Douglass and finished at 12 under par for two days, nine behind winners J.C. Snead and Gibby Gilbert.

A visitor to Diamondback is very likely to find Coody hitting balls on the range. It is still a joy to watch his rhythmic swing, even at age 75. It is the swing of a champion; a Masters Champion.

Poster promoting a tournament in Odessa

A Tale of Two Cities

"We are isolated out here and have to create our own entertainment."

Mickey Jones

Odessa, Texas

Midland and Odessa are only 20 miles apart but a long way from anyplace else. There is an intense rivalry, like all good Texas towns so close in proximity, but because they are set off from the rest of the world, there is also much cooperation.

Before the world became aware of the Permian Basin through the popular movie and television show *Friday Night Lights*, the two towns enjoyed hosting big time golfing events in the form of the Odessa Pro-Am at Odessa Country Club and the Texas State Amateur and even a Ryder Cup dress rehearsal event at Midland Country Club.

Mickey Jones is a former president of the Texas Golf Association and grew up playing golf at Odessa Country Club. His father served on the tournament committee for many years at the Odessa Pro-Am while Bobby French of Midland Country Club performed a lot of the public relations duties. It was a showcase of cooperation between the two cities.

There is a short film about the pro-am in 1966 with French narrating and sponsored by a local bank in Midland. French mentions the economic impact of the event with the large crowds coming out to see Dean Martin and his partner, Don Cherry. The film shows Charles Coody winning the tournament with his partner Richard Patton and the unmistakable swing of Lee Trevino, an unknown at that time and playing with Dick Martin of Dallas.

Mickey Jones said:

Bobby French was a Midland guy who now lives in Palm Springs. He always played with Bo Wininger who won it one time with Billy Maxwell. Wininger and Maxwell both claimed to be from Odessa at one time. I don't think they ever actually lived here... But the guys like French who helped put on the event knew it was good for the community but they didn't have the ways to measure it back then. I would guess it meant about $2 million to the community at that time.

French was a good player in his own right, winning the prestigious West Texas Amateur in 1949 and 1950. "I went out one year with the little pro, Hal McCommas, and we had a ball," Dallas amateur golfing legend Bob Rawlins said. "We played with Bo Wininger and Bobby French. Both of them had Hollywood looks and Bobby had more money than God."

"We never did too much good," Rawlins, aka *Dark Cloud* said. "Those guys were just too good out there back then."

Jones was a little too young to ever play in the event that ended in 1969 with Maxwell and Richard Ellis winning the final tournament, but he caddied in it and got to see the Dean Martin show from the front row.

I caddied for Don Cherry one year. And we were on number 15 which was into the wind. I knew how far he (Cherry) could hit it. He was a good player and Dean Martin was his partner. So he said, "can I get a three-iron there" and I said you better hit a two-iron. So he said I am going to hit a three-iron and he hits it about six feet high under the wind on the green and says it was just a stock three-iron. As we are walking up the fairway, Dean came over and whispered to me that Cherry could be a little hard headed.

Jones said that Martin was a nice guy and the golfer every young boy in Odessa wanted to caddy for during the pro-am. Jones' boyhood friend Ricky Fitzmeyer got the job and the perks of having a gallery full of pretty, well dressed women.

Jones said:

Every time, on the first hole, Martin would send Ricky for a coke. And then, with everyone crowded around the tee, he would take a big swig of coke and then spit it out. "Why, that's straight coke," he would say and the gallery would just howl with laughter. The drinking thing with Dean Martin was just an act. He just loved to play golf.

Jones also fondly remembers the duo of Don January and his amateur friend Dick Jennings of Lubbock. They won the tournament in 1960 and both are still golfing in their golden years. A few years ago, Jones said, he played at Jennings' home course in Lubbock when Jennings made a hole in one that was his 26th or 27th ace. Jones said:

> He is a tax lawyer and good friend of January. He has a funny swing but can repeat it. One year they are playing with Cherry and Martin when January tried to get Dean to drink a beer and he wouldn't. That may have been the day that Doug Sanders came out to watch. I think he was trying to sell Martin something so he flew into town but wasn't even playing. Some said he just came into town to play gin rummy back at the clubhouse.

Jones said that at the end, as the PGA Tour began to crack down on players going to the Odessa Pro-Am instead of a tour event opposite the British Open, the tournament was shut down because it would have been significantly diminished.

> I respect the people behind it because they were not going to have it if they could not have it in a big way that people were accustomed to. In its heyday, you had the tournament winners to draw the golfing gallery and you had Dean Martin to bring in the people who just loved entertainment... And that's the thing about Midland and Odessa; we are isolated out here and have to create our own entertainment. That has been the case through the years with lots of good minor league baseball and things like that.

Both towns are known for superb junior college golf programs. Odessa College has won eight national championships with six of those coming in years 1959 through 1965. In that era the team was coached by Jimmy Russell who hosted the first junior college national tournament at the Odessa Country Club. His tradition is being continued by current coach Paul Chavez who led the team to national titles in 2004 and 2005.

Midland College got into the mix of top junior college golf when it hired West Texas legend Delnor Poss in 1980 to coach its team. Poss has led his team to 22 straight national tournament appearances and taken home four championships. He also established a Scotland connection through former players Andrew Coltart and Guy Redford and the current team of 10 features six players from the United Kingdom.

Poss has done many things in a full life that includes basketball playing and officiating. He once threw Bobby Knight out of a game in El Paso and used to shoot hoops with football legend Sammy Baugh.

Redford, now the head golf professional at Dundonald Links near Troon in Scotland, remembers one incident that captures Poss' personality.

"Many years ago, we're going to a tournament and about five miles from the course Coach said let me out," Redford said. "He then began jogging and said he would meet us at the course. He is such a great guy."

Midland Country Club has hosted three state amateurs in the years 1965, 1971, and 1997. Those tournaments were won by Randy Petri of Austin, Bruce Lietzke of Beaumont, and Ed Books of Georgetown. It even hosted a dress rehearsal for the Ryder Cup in 1955.

Texas golf historian Frances Trimble wrote about the special event that was held at a still new Midland Country Club. Built in 1950 with the design by Texas Golf Hall of Fame architect Ralph Plummer, the club had some influential members like Eddie Chiles of Fort Worth, a successful oilman who once coined this advertising slogan for his drilling company; *Don't have an oil well? Get one. You'll love doing business with Western.* Chiles and company arranged a challenge match between the U.S. team captained by Chick Harbert and a hand-picked squad chosen by Jimmy Demaret.

The Americans were on their way to the West Coast where they would defeat the British team captained by Dais Rees, 8-4. The American team that year included Cary Middlecoff, Chandler Harper, Tommy Bolt, Doug Ford, Jackie Burke, Jr., Jerry Barber, and Marty Furgol. Demaret's team was no push over with Lord Byron Nelson, Mike Souchak, Vic Ghezzi, Al Besselink, Fred Hawkins, Bob Moncrief, and Odessa Pro-Am regulars Billy Maxwell, Don Cherry, and Bo Wininger.

There is no record of who won those matches but does it really matter? It was just another example of folks in the Permian Basin creating their own entertainment.

SECTION III: SOUTH TEXAS

I'm telling you, pal, put your shirt on.

Tommy Burke
Corpus Christi, Texas

CORPUS CHRISTI
COUNTRY CLUB

Corpus Christi, Texas

Logo for Corpus Christi Country Club

The Throwback Course

"What we were looking for was more of a restoration than a true renovation."

Richard Luikens

Conroe, Texas

One of the features of the old beer and barbecue circuit was the nine-hole course. The nine-hole tracks sported two sets of tees to give the holes some variety and the courses were prevalent throughout the state. Most, like the old circuit, have disappeared or been expanded to 18 holes. One notable exception is the Conroe Country Club just 30 miles north of Houston.

At about the same time as Houston wildcatter George Strake was discovering a major oil field near Conroe in 1931, a group of local businessmen decided to start a country club. This was the same year that Billy Burke won the U.S. Open at the Inverness Club in Toledo, Ohio, in a marathon 72-hole playoff over George Von Elm. It was also two years before the Augusta National Golf Club in Georgia opened for play. The founders decided to bring in John Bredemus, later known as the Donald Ross of Texas golf, to design a nine-hole golf course.

Fast forward almost 80 years and another group of Conroe businessmen, this time on the board of the country club and with the approval of the members, decided to spend almost two million dollars to restore the club to its original design. "What we were looking for was more of a restoration than a true renovation," Conroe Country Club member Richard Luikens said. "I looked at the golf course all of these years and thought, when we do something to the course, we need to do it right and keep the old style feel."

In essence, Conroe Country Club is an old fashioned, small-town country club that has clung to its roots while being swallowed by the Houston suburbia. In the 1950s, before the Champions Golf Club was built, Conroe Country Club was the first golf course north of the original site of Pine Forest Golf Club at the intersection of Loop 610 and Shepherd Drive. Considering the plethora of courses now in operation in Montgomery County alone, it is hard to imagine such a time before the rapid growth of greater Houston.

Often described as a walk back in time, the club is unique among courses in the Houston area. It is owned by its 300 members and has no golf professional or club manager. There are no tee times required and the members have never wanted to expand to 18 holes. Located two miles from downtown on the southeast corner of the busy intersection of Highway 105 and Loop 336, the country club sits back about a half mile from the highway and is generally unnoticed by any passerby.

Liukens said:

> The drive into the club is nice because it is somewhat hidden from view. You talk to people in town and tell them where the course is and they will always say that they never knew there was a golf course there. Once you turn into the club, you don't see anything for the first third of a mile or so. You drive through a grove of trees and other vegetation and then into a clearing and there is the clubhouse and the course.

To improve the course and the clubhouse, Luikens and other members researched the history of the club and found valuable information. Luikens added:

> Our club was originally started in 1931. We got confirmation of its origins from the Conroe Courier newspaper. One of the articles talks about the fairways being graded and there is an aerial photo with it. This is from June of 1930 so we found concrete proof of when the course was built.

After looking at the old photographs, the changes were purposefully subtle. The routing of the holes remains the same as in 1931. "The aerial photo from 1930 may be one of the clearest that we have," Luikens said. "We said that the guy must have been up in a helium balloon or something to take the pictures. It shows the cleared areas for the fairways because at that time the grass had not been planted."

The first of the changes was to lessen the slopes of the greens. This was done to accommodate a new and better strain of Bermuda grass that fosters a faster surface. The greens were reseeded with Mini Verde, the "latest and the greatest" of the new Bermuda grasses and the type recently used at such high profile courses as the TPC Stadium Course in Jacksonville, Florida and Eastlake, site of the Tour Championship, in Atlanta. "Some of our members said that the holes looked different but that the shots required were similar," Luikens said.

Another feature of the course dramatically changed was the tee boxes. The tees were better lined up with the shape of the holes and designed to have a more square or rectangular look. This also reflects the style of the 1930s and 1940s time period.

Restoring the course to the days of John Bredemus required some thought as to what might be the signature feature of his designs. A beloved eccentric praised by none other than Harvey Penick in his *Little Red Book*, Bredemus designed more than thirty courses in Texas during the 1920s and 1930s. The two best known are Colonial in Fort Worth and Memorial Park in Houston. Using Colonial as an example, his creative use of the dogleg on par-four holes stands out.

> *His toughest hole at Colonial is number five that runs along the Trinity River on the right side of the fairway. It's a dogleg from left to right. It compares to our number seven hole which doglegs the same way to an uphill green with a severely sloped fairway to the left. You have to hit a cut shot to hold the fairway and then you have the uphill second shot. It is our hardest hole.*

Though not long at 6,600 yards from the tips, the Conroe course has a variety of doglegs and other challenging features. Golfers as accomplished as former state amateur champion Robert McKinney have praised it for the variety of shots required each round. McKinney, a Houston architect, was chosen to design the new clubhouse.

Again Liukens said:

> *With the new clubhouse, we wanted to have a nice new locker room and a view of the golf course. We now have a big porch on the back of the clubhouse that has a nice view of the ninth hole, especially the green, so that you can watch others finish after your round... It's an old style building because that is something that we wanted. It looks as if it was built in the 1930s or 1940s. We have a nice bricked fireplace and pretty high ceilings.*

The new clubhouse is essentially the same size as the original one that served as the focal point of Conroe society for many decades.

The original clubhouse was built in 1934. It was a two-story building with an original cost of $7,000. The original square footage was about five to six thousand square feet. The upstairs was the ballroom and it was at least 3,000 square feet and in its day it was the place for all social functions in Conroe and Montgomery County.

Perhaps the most enjoyable part of the restoration process has been the way that it was financed. "What is great is that we did not have to assess the membership. We were able to use other funds from the sale of assets and so forth. We have 300 members. Not all of them play golf but a lot enjoy the clubhouse and other things at the club."

In today's world, that makes Conroe Country Club indeed unique.

The 9th green and clubhouse at Conroe Country Club

Christmas in April

"We believe that our tournament is the oldest match play championship in Texas."

Danny Nichol

Conroe, Texas

On Monday of the last week of April each year, Curt Maddux gets a phone call from his friend and golfing companion Scott Loving. "It's Christmas time again," Loving says. "Are you at the course because I am headed that way!"

Loving and Maddux, both grown men and successful in business, are as excited as two young boys on Christmas Day. They are headed to Conroe Country Club for their favorite week of the year. It's the first day of practice rounds for the club's annual invitational.

While most tournaments on the late, great beer and barbecue circuit have faded away or changed to milder best-ball formats, the Conroe tournament is still going strong after more than 70 years. It is an invitational in the truest sense of the word.

"We send out the invitations in late February and people are at the club, standing in line to pay their entry fee, on the day they receive them," Maddux said. "We have even had people drive to the club from their homes on the day they receive it in the mail and still be too late to get in."

Both Maddux and Loving are scratch golfers who have won the tournament in the past. Maddux won in 2004 and has been runner up twice while Loving won three years in a row in 2006, 2007, and 2008. Maddux is also the tournament chairman and has been for the last 12 years. He accepted the job from fellow Conroe Country Club member Danny Nichol, who ran the tournament the previous seven years.

"We believe that our tournament is the oldest match play championship in Texas," Nichol said. "It started in 1931 and we have had some of the best players in the state play each year. Some of the top players who have played here are Miller Barber, Billy Maxwell, Rocky Thompson, Mark Hopkins, Jacky Cupit, Homero Blancas, Richard Crawford, and Joe Conrad."

Nichol grew up in Conroe and played on one of the many state high school championship teams that the community has had through the years. He began playing at Conroe Country Club in 1952 and has been involved in the tournament in some capacity each year.

Back in those days, the tournament was a big deal because the closest golf course was Pine Forest in Houston where the University of Houston hosted the All America college tournament... All of the University of Houston players used to play in it back then. I remember one year, around 1960, when Blancas came and won the qualifier to get into the championship flight and then won the putting contest, the long drive contest and the tournament. He won everything there was to win. I played a practice round with him then because I would just hang out and ask good players if I could play with them.

Some of the Houston area golfers even call the Conroe invitational South Texas' version of the Masters. Instead of a drive down Magnolia Lane, the participants drive down the entrance to a club that was started around 1930 and designed by the legendary John Bredemus. During tournament week, the course and its grounds are resplendent and a large banner welcomes the golfers. "It's a long standing tradition for our club and everyone supports it," Maddux said. "I started out as a kid working as a volunteer to keep the grounds neat and now I have about 30 such volunteers helping."

The tournament committee also runs the tournament in a manner that rivals the ruling bodies in Augusta. Players no longer qualify because the championship flight and first flight players are handpicked and seeded by Maddux and his committee. Both flights of 16 are made up of scratch or better handicaps. "There are some bruised egos but that's part of the appeal," Maddux said. "If you think you should be in the championship flight, prove it by winning the first flight. A lot of guys play their way in that way."

One player is exempt into the championship flight each year and that is the defending champion. Sandy Pierce of Houston, one of many fine players at the Champions Golf Club, won the tournament in 2010 for his second title. A previous winner of the club championship at Champions, Pierce also won at Conroe in 2005.

Van Gillen is a long-time member and outstanding amateur. He played at the University of Houston in the early 1970s and has won the tournament five times, most recently in 2001. He gets just as excited as Maddux and Loving each year. "We are fortunate that the economy in Conroe hasn't gone away," Gillen said. "A lot of our members don't play much golf but they like to come out to watch the tournament. The community also supports it."

Gillen cites his wins over Loving as his favorite memories through the years. "Scott is a good bit younger than me and a very good player. In a couple of the years that I won, I was able to beat Scott during the semifinals."

The tournament format can be grueling since the winner must win four matches. The golfers play one match on Friday, one on Saturday, and one or two on Sunday, depending on the result of the morning match.

Crowds tend to get large on the weekends because of another innovation Nichol implemented several years back. In the oil business since 1978, Nichol decided to ask some of his associates, The Oilies, who don't play serious golf, to crank up some grills behind the eighth green and feed the spectators. Nothing helps bring out a crowd like free food, especially such healthy items as fried ribs.

Nichol, who won in 1964, said above all, it is the keen competition that drives the tournament. The names of players who have not won the tournament are impressive. Consider former state amateur and mid-amateur champion Robert McKinney of Houston. He has played in the tournament for years and finally won his first match last year.

"You better put on your birdie hat when you go to the Conroe invitational," McKinney said. "There are some guys who are just really hard to beat on that course. It's a good and fair course which tests you with all kinds of shots but just the familiarity of some of the guys is an advantage. There are a lot of good players from Conroe."

One amateur from Houston who has won the tournament twice is Tommy Cruse. Even at age 78, Cruse has a deep and rich East Texas accent that only an actor of the caliber of Robert Duvall could possibly imitate.

A native of Jacksonville, Cruse is a successful insurance man who has lived most of his adult life in Houston. A short and slight man who has always worn glasses, to some he might look more at home at the library than on a golf course. By his own account, Cruse won more than 20 beer and barbecue tournaments during his younger years. He played his college golf at University of Houston in the early 1950s and thought about turning pro. After watching Ben Hogan, who was the best professional at that time and making only about $25,000 per year, Cruse decided to stay an amateur. Cruse began to sell insurance and play the barbecue circuit in the Houston area and back home in East Texas. Though Cruse won often, he had to work hard to win at Conroe, the biggest invitational tournament in the Houston area.

The quality of the field has always been strong, as Cruse remembers. "One of my best memories at Conroe is that I beat Bobby Nichols, 6 and 5, in the morning match and then Babe Hiskey in the afternoon match," Cruse said. "Then I lost the next morning to Rocky Thompson who I believe won the tournament that year."

Although Nichols hails from Kentucky, he played his college golf at Texas A&M and later beat Jack Nicklaus and Arnold Palmer to win the 1964 PGA Championship. Hiskey and Thompson also won on the PGA and Champions Tour. Nichols is just one of many fine players who never won the Conroe tournament played on its manicured nine-hole course.

Miller Barber remembers beating short game guru Phil Rodgers at Conroe during the late 1950s when Rodgers was the NCAA individual champion at University of Houston. Rodgers now teaches at the Del Mar Grand resort in California and won five times on the tour. He "owned" Nicklaus when they competed as junior golfers and won the NCAA in the only year he played for the Cougars in 1958. He is also known for losing a 36-hole playoff to Bob Charles for the 1963 British Open championship.

"You would have thought I shot him or something," Barber said. "Nobody beat him in those days but I got him that day. He just had this look on his face, kind of like disbelief, that I will never forget."

Bruised egos, it seems, are also a tradition at the Conroe invitational.

Trophy Golf

"I didn't get any of the money, only the trophy."

Joe Conrad

San Antonio, Texas

On no less authority than Mr. John Paul Cain, *Smoky Joe* Conrad is said to have made the longest putt ever in competition and it came at the home of golf, the Old Course at St. Andrews, Scotland. "It was 97 steps or 291 feet on one of those double greens," Conrad said. "So I was obviously on the wrong part of it. The 15th hole was where it happened."

Holing a 97-yard putt is something hard to forget, even after almost 60 years. That particular Walker Cup was the last one where the American team traveled by ship and Conrad remembers fellow Texan Don Cherry not only singing from the steps of the Old Course clubhouse, but every night on the ship sailing across the Atlantic.

A native of San Antonio, Conrad played on the winning team of the Walker Cup that week, along with Cherry of Wichita Falls and a great amateur named Harvie Ward. It was during those matches that he got his nickname *Smoky Joe*, by the Brits, presumably because of his Texas roots.

Two weeks later, Conrad won the British Amateur at Royal Lytham and St. Anne's on the west coast of England, just up the road from Royal Birkdale and Royal Liverpool (Hoylake), two other British Open venues still on the rotation. Before winning in England, Conrad won the Mexican Amateur, the Southern Amateur at Lakewood in Dallas, and the Texas Amateur Championship in 1951 at Corsicana Country Club. All are very prestigious titles and Conrad is the only Texan to ever win the British Amateur. But it was a tournament win in Dallas in 1948 that Conrad remembers the most.

"Winning the Southern Amateur at Lakewood over Gay Brewer in 1953 is what probably got me picked for the Walker Cup," Conrad said. "But beating Dick Martin in the Dallas Public Links Championship in 1948 is one that I remember well."

Only 18 and contemplating his college plans, Conrad was in Dallas to visit the University of North Texas. He was staying with L.M. Crannell, another UNT golfer who won some big amateur tournaments during the same time period.

"Nobody knew me so L.M.'s dad bought me in the Calcutta for only $25," Conrad said. "We were playing Tenison Park and Dick Martin owned that place back then. Well we made it to the finals and I was one down after 18 holes and told Mr. Crannell that I'm doing pretty good, being only one down."

Conrad said he went with the Crannells to eat a hamburger at the little drive-in place near the second tee of the East Course at Tenison. "Then I eagled the first hole of the afternoon round, the par five that runs down the side of the road, and that pulled me even with him. I ended up winning two and one."

So, was your take of the Calcutta money pretty good?
Conrad answered:

Oh no, I didn't get any money, only the trophy. I may have also won a set of irons or something but it is really sad what happened with the Calcutta. They had Titantic Thompson and some hustlers there who had bet heavily on Martin and all of the money was in checks. None of those checks cleared so that Mr. Crannell didn't make much money if any. The next year they policed the Calcutta better by having some kind of pari-mutuel betting each day.

Conrad played in his share of barbecue tournaments, mostly in West Texas with some impressive wins at Plainview over local star Jack Williams and then Lubbock over Bo Wininger. He also played several years at the Odessa Pro-Am with San Antonio pro Warren Smith of Oak Hills Country Club. Conrad said they never finished higher than fourth in that tournament.

After winning the 1951 State Amateur, Conrad did something that shows a lot about his character and determination. Having grown up in San Antonio and playing in every Texas State Junior since he was 13, he was going to try one more time to win it later that summer of 1951. "Back then, you could play in the State Junior until you were 21 so I gave it another go and finally won it."

Invited to play in the Colonial the following year, Conrad was paired the first day with Ben Hogan and Lloyd Mangrum, two tough as nails Texans. "They said, 'Hi Lloyd and hi Ben' and that was about it for the day," Conrad recalled. "And that was the first year they started allowing spectators to line the right side of the fairway. There were people lining both sides of the fairway and I was so nervous that I duck hooked my first tee shot and hit someone. Then I hooked my second shot on the third hole and hit someone else. They had to call an ambulance out to look after him."

"We finally get around to the 10th and I hit too good a drive and ended up in the creek in the middle of the fairway. I go on to make a double bogey and I was playing bad and just so embarrassed."

Conrad finally makes it in and shoots an 83.

"I was keeping Mangrum's card and Hogan was keeping mine. He handed me my card and I said 'you didn't total the scores.' He said he didn't have to do that but I asked if he would."

Hogan, after adding up all of the scores turned and handed the card to Conrad.

"He said, 'My God Joe, I thought you were hitting it pretty good. Where did you have your trouble?'"

It was another story of how Hogan could be so singularly focused on his own game. Conrad later played in the Colonial as a pro in 1957 and finished in the top 20. "I actually led the Colonial for two days," Conrad said with a chuckle. "I shot 68 the first round and then the second round was rained out."

He was only a touring pro for a couple of years before becoming a club pro, first at Canyon Creek and then his own driving range in San Antonio. During his brief touring pro days, he remembers playing a lot of tournaments in California with Charlie Sifford, the first African-American to win on the PGA Tour. This was before the infamous *Caucasian Only* rule was rescinded and California was more accommodating than the rest of the country. Sifford is a good friend of Joe Jimizez, a good player from San Antonio that Conrad has known well for many years.

"I guess I just played my best golf as an amateur," Conrad said.

Perhaps a bit of an understatement since in addition to winning the Southern Amateur at Lakewood in 1953, he successfully defended the title the next year at Memphis Country Club and also won the Trans Mississippi Amateur at Kansas City Country Club in 1953.

He played on national championship teams at UNT with Billy Maxwell and Don January. Short and stocky like Maxwell, Conrad said people sometimes confused them. "Except at the pay window," Conrad said. "Billy really did well as a pro."

One additional treasure of his win at the British Amateur is a splendid piece written by the esteemed Herbert Warren Wind for the June 13th issue of *Sports Illustrated*.

> *At the Royal Lytham and St. Anne's Golf Club, that weather-beaten links off the Irish Sea above Liverpool where Bobby Jones in 1926 captured his first of three British Opens, Joe Conrad, a small, compact, steady and impassive 25-year-old Air Force lieutenant from San Antonio, gained the first major triumph of his career last Saturday by winning the 60th edition of the British Amateur Golf Championship.*

In a special profile later that year by Wind, Conrad was lauded for winning the British Amateur in a funny way by his mother. "I just can't believe that little guy going way over there and winning something big like that."

Believe it because his name is etched permanently on that trophy. And trophies last longer than money.

Krueger, Kite and Crenshaw

Crenshaw loves to tell and hear stories about Dudley Krueger."

Billy Clagett

Austin, Texas

The Firecracker Open at Lions Municipal Golf Course in Austin is no longer a true barbecue tournament but it is still going strong. Won by the likes of Ben Crenshaw and Tom Kite, the Firecracker Open has always drawn a talented field. The tournament was first played in 1946 and has not missed a year with Stratton Nolen winning the 65th playing in 2011.

In its early days, the tournament was known as the Texas Public Links Golf Association Championship. It changed to the Austin Golf Association Invitational Championship and then in 1950 became known as the Fourth of July Championship. The tournament moved to the Morris Williams golf course when it opened in 1964 and was played there for three years before moving back to the course Austin folks just call *Muni*.

In 1967, the tournament became The Firecracker Golf Festival Championship and is now known as The Firecracker Open. Still played at Lion's, the P.W. Curry trophy is entrusted to the winner each year.

Besides Crenshaw who won it twice in 1969 and 1971, and Kite who won in 1968, other notable winners include current tour player Omar Uresti in 1986 and 1989 and former state amateur champion Randy Petri in 1959,1962, and 1965. Petri won the state amateur in 1965 at Midland Country Club and also played the PGA Tour for a short stint. One other winner well known in Texas golfing circles was Billy Penn in 1957. Penn was the former director of the Texas Golf Association and passed away in 2003.

Lions pro Lloyd Morrison said:

We have to shut it off at 165 players because Lions is a short course and it is hard to move more people than that around. It is a 54-hole medal play tournament and we have quite a waiting list each year to get in... It used to have a Calcutta but that was dropped when it moved to Morris Williams. We still have the barbecue and everyone has a good time.

Morrison said players still come from all over Texas but the bulk of entrants are from the Austin area. The Lions municipal course is one of the busiest anywhere with approximately 70,000 rounds played on it each year. It is also embroiled in an ongoing controversy with the University of Texas, which owns the land and has been inferring that it may not renew the lease in 2019.

In the clubhouse at Lions is perhaps the most extensive scrapbook of Austin golf in existence. It was put together by Mildred Neil who passed away in 2005. A labor of love, the scrapbook, Morrison said, is three feet wide with more than 300 pages of local golf history from 1939 until the late 1980s.

The man who has won the tournament most often is Billy Clagett of Austin. A retired club pro and golf cart salesman, Clagett first won the Firecracker in 1988 and most recently in 2001. He has taken home the Curry trophy a total of six times.

"To get my name on that trophy with people like Billy Penn and Dudley Krueger, not to mention Crenshaw and Kite, is quite an honor," Clagett said. "It is a special tournament because it has all of the good young players and folks like me who still want to compete. And there is always a good gallery out to watch."

Krueger is an Austin legend who won the first tournament in 1946 and again in 1951. He was a janitor at UT and known for his colorful ways and golfing skills. "Crenshaw loves to hear and tell stories about Dudley Krueger," Clagett said.

Famous Last Names

"This book has been collected and arranged with love by Jesse Westfall."

Jesse Westfall

Corpus Christi, Texas

It has been more than 25 years since the last playing of the Corpus Christi Country Club Invitational. What began in 1936 and continued for almost 50 years was a prestigious match play event that featured a 36-hole final match. Attracting players from throughout the state, the tournament started with a qualifier on Wednesday that seeded the 32-man championship flight and then continued with single matches on Thursday and Friday and two matches Saturday for the winners to reach the finals.

Until 1967, the tournament was played on the original country club layout that was near the port and adjacent to a large refinery. It, like Conroe Country Club, was designed by John Bredemus. Rick Rogers is an attorney in Corpus Christi and a board member with the Texas Golf Association. He grew up playing the original country club course and remembers working one summer at the refinery. He later won the invitational three times and lost two others in the finals.

Rogers said:

I played in my first invitational in 1963 or 1964 when I was 19 or 20. I was at Texas Tech when I played in my first finals match and lost to Jerry Don Barrier, who was a fine player... One summer I worked at the refinery near the old course and played every day. At lunchtime, I would run over to the country club and eat a hamburger and then at four, when I got off work, I would go play with (Tommy) *Burke until dark.*

Now 84, Tommy Burke was the pro at the country club from 1958 until 1988. He grew up in Houston and his cousin Jackie is the irascible founder of the Champions Golf Club. With the vitality and memory of a much younger man, Burke still plays or gives lessons every day.

"Let me tell you about J.T. Jamison," Burke said of the winner of the 1947 and 1948 tournaments. "He was about six-foot and weighed 270. He was a land man for Sun Oil Company from Midland... They got up a big money game one time where he played the best ball of the Bauer sisters, Marlene and Alice. He beat them one up and they played for $25,000."

The Bauer sisters were charter members of Ladies Professional Golf Association. Alice passed away in 2002 but Marlene, a winner of 25 LPGA events, lives in California with her husband Ernie Vossler, a winner of many Texas barbecue tournaments and the medalist in 1948 at Corpus Christi.

Vossler is indicative of the caliber of players who traveled to Corpus Christi in the early years of the event. Earl Stewart was medalist in the 1941 tournament won by Lonnie Wendland of Corpus Christi. Wendland would go on to win the tournament again in 1950 and 1951.

In 1945, Wally Ulrich defeated Raleigh Selby of Kilgore in the finals. Ulrich was the 1943 NCAA champion from Carleton College in Minnesota and also won the Mexican Amateur in 1945. He turned pro and won one PGA Tour event.

Dr. C.K. Emery won his first of three titles in 1954 and his son Charlie, who played college golf at SMU, won the tournament once in 1966. "I never caddied at the tournament when I was a kid but I remember going out to watch Dr. Emery," Rogers said. "He was a fierce competitor and had a fine short game."

Burke agrees with that assessment but delightfully recalls the Achilles heel of the doctor's game:

He was notorious for missing very short putts. He could make the 15 and 20 foot putts but would yip the short ones. So one day he is headed out to the putting green with his putter and sleeve of balls and one of our members says to me, "there goes doc out to practice gimmes."

The only man to win the invitational four times was John Garrett of Houston. An ophthalmologist, Garrett still plays at River Oaks Country Club. He won the tournament in 1957, 1960, 1962, and 1973.

"John Garrett was one heck of a player," Burke said. "If he had turned pro in the mid 1950s he would have been better than Arnold Palmer. He was tall and strong and could hit a driver off the deck better than anyone I have ever seen. He was very long back then."

Another top amateur during the 1960s who hailed from Corpus Christi was Richard Yates. Now living in Gonzales, Yates won the 1961 invitational over Walter Fondren of Houston. Fondren passed away in 2010 and was known as the million dollar quarterback for UT in the late 1950s since his family was one of founders of the Humble Oil Company that is now Exxon.

Yates lost to Garrett in the 1960 final but won the Texas amateur at the Corpus Christi Country Club in 1963. With Rogers caddying for him, Yates' bid for a repeat state amateur win was thwarted in 1964 by Marty Fleckman in the finals at Willow Brook Country Club in Tyler.

Robert Trent Jones designed the present Corpus Christi Country Club that opened for play in 1968. The winner of the invitational that year was Bill Evans and he was followed in 1969 by Rik Massengale. George Tucker of Midland won in 1970 while Corpus Christi players Stan Altgelt and Ham Rogers, Rick's brother, won in 1971 and 1972.

Tim Carlton, the recent runner up to John Grace in the Texas state senior championship at Odessa Country Club, grew up in Corpus Christi and won the invitational in 1974 over Art Leon of Dallas. Leon's daughter Taylor currently plays on the LPGA Tour.

Rick Rogers won his first of three titles in 1976. He won again in 1977 and in 1980. The finals match in 1980 was an epic battle with fellow country club member Jay Kent, who was going for a third consecutive championship after winning in 1978 and 1979.

All tied after 36 holes, Rogers and Kent went into sudden death with Rogers prevailing on the 38th hole. "That match was the best for me because there was a big crowd and my dad was walking with us," Rogers said. "I hit a wood from the rough on that final hole to about 10 feet and made the putt for an eagle to win."

Kent would win his third championship the following year.

Rogers remembers another aspect of the tournament that was unique. The winner was presented a special scrapbook prepared by Jesse Westfall at the closing ceremony. Rogers said:

> She was a good golfer who loved the game and had to quit playing because of some ailments. She would prepare the folder that had the opening announcements and articles from the paper during the tournament. She would even have people in the gallery sign congratulatory notes. It was a tradition to get her book before you received the trophy and it always said, "This book has been collected and arranged with love by Jesse Westfall."

Sadly, Jesse Westfall passed away in the late 1970s and with that her tradition ended. But before the tournament went away, it did have its lighter moments.

The winner in 1982 was Andrew Magee of Dallas who played and won on the PGA Tour and is now a popular commentator on The Golf Channel. Known for his zaniness during his younger years, Magee was almost disqualified from the tournament that year for taking his shirt off during play. Obviously trying to beat the heat of a Fourth of July tournament in South Texas, Magee was nevertheless politely asked to put on his shirt.

"He asked me if I was asking him or telling him," Burke said. "I'm telling you, pal, put your shirt on."

Magee quickly put on his shirt.

Corpus Christi attorney Rick Rogers and family circa early 1980s

A Greek God

"He was like a Greek god or something,"

Jim Todd

Lufkin, Texas

Marty Fleckman was a fitness freak long before it became fashionable on tour. When he was playing the beer and barbecue circuit during his college days at the University of Houston, he said he never went to the Calcutta because "those sometimes went into the wee hours and I was in training so I didn't hang around."

Even in his 60s, the handsome Fleckman looks years younger than his age and tries to eat right and drink good water. "He used to bring big barrels out to Bear Creek to fill them up with our well water because he didn't trust the Houston water," longtime pro Rick Forester said.

Fleckman's current fitness routine is still Spartan. "I work out everyday. I am a very regimented individual. I try to stay healthy and eat the right things. I live only about 300 yards from my office so I spend very little time driving. I have a good trainer and she keeps me going with the proper exercises and I hit balls about five or six times a week."

So it wasn't surprising that Jim Todd of Lufkin was a little awe-struck as a high school kid when he first saw Fleckman hitting balls on the range at tiny Cherokee Country Club in Jackonsville.

"He was like a Greek god or something," Todd said. "I had never seen anyone hit a golf ball like him."

It was at that time, while Fleckman was in college, that he won just about everything on the barbecue circuit before turning his attention to national amateur events and winning those as well. He won the Briarwood Invitational in 1963 and 1964 with a State Amateur title across town in

Tyler at Willow Brook Country Club in 1964. Then in 1965, he added the Center Invitational to his list of wins.

A.J. Triggs remembers a story about Fleckman's fitness during the 1964 State Amateur. "He stayed with us that week and my house was a good ways from the course, across town," Triggs said. "One of the early rounds, he went to hit practice balls down in the low area of the course and I told him that I had to leave about 5 pm to get home. He said to go ahead, that he would jog home later and he did."

But even before winning the three tournaments in Tyler, the stocky and long hitting athlete from Port Arthur, had a lot of people's attention. Jim Fetters, a fellow native of Port Arthur said:

He could really play. He hit it so far with the hook and was a great wedge player. He had great heart and great grit... I took Fleckman to his first beer and barbecue tournament when he was only 14 or 15 and he hits a drive and a sand wedge into the hole. It was his first hole at Marshall.

Though he was in training, Fleckman said he was always curious to see who bought him in the Calcutta the next day when the tournament began. "You always wanted to know who bought you, who owns you," he said. "I was never in a situation like Homero Blancas where he had to win the tournament for his buyers to get their money back. There was a lot of East Texas oil money up there and it was a fun deal."

East Texas wasn't the only place Fleckman enjoyed playing in the early and mid 1960s. He won the Odessa Pro-Am twice, both times as the amateur. He won in 1963 with his pro from Port Arthur, Ned Johnson, and then again in 1965 with Babe Hiskey.

"I remember Fleckman carrying his pro partner," Odessa Country Club member Ronald Crain said. "He played better than most of the pros that year."

After all of his success at the University of Houston where the Cougars were winning the national championship regularly under coach Dave Williams, Fleckman turned his attention to the big national amateur events.

Fleckman said:

I wasn't in any hurry to turn pro. I lacked six hours for my degree so I stayed an extra semester. I had made the Walker Cup team and wanted to play in it at Royal St. George's in England. This was in 1967. It was before the U.S. Open because the week after the Walker Cup was the British Amateur at Formby. So I stayed and played in the British Amateur and then went back to Connecticut and stayed with a friend to try to qualify for the U.S. Open at Baltusrol in New Jersey... I qualified and then led it after the first and third rounds. I played with Casper the last day when he shot 80 and Nicklaus ended up winning using a Bullseye putter painted white that he called the White Fang.

Fleckman rebounded from his disappointment at the U.S. Open to win the Northeast Amateur the next week at Wannamoisett Country Club near Providence, Rhode Island, a Donald Ross course with a par 69 and some super slick greens. He also won the Eastern Amateur at Elizabeth Manor in Portsmouth, Virginia in 1966. Fleckman said he was also medalist two years running in the Western Amateur, first with a 65 at Point O Woods in Michigan in 1965 and then a 67 at Pinehurst #2 the next year. His round at Pinehurst is memorable because he played the four par-three's in eight strokes with an ace, two birdies and a par.

Most people of a certain age remember Fleckman's lead at the U.S. Open, but most forget that he was in the same position the next year at the PGA Championship at Pecan Valley in San Antonio.

I fondly remember the U.S. Open and the PGA. In 1967 at the U.S. Open, I was an amateur who couldn't win any money so I went out to win the tournament. And then I bogeyed three of the first four holes and tried to attack the course. You can't attack a U.S. Open course. So I learned from that and used it at the PGA the next year and just tried to play the golf course. I had one thing on my mind and that was not to shoot 80 the last day like I did at the U.S. Open.

Playing what the course would give him; Fleckman remained in contention at the PGA until the very end.

A lot of people don't remember that I had a one shot lead with five to play but bogeyed three holes to lose. Julius Boros won it and I finished third or fourth. It's real ironic because I gave up a spot in Masters in 1968 to turn pro but my high finish in the PGA got me into the 1969 Masters. I missed the cut.

The irony at the 1969 Masters was also that the winner, George Archer, was an amateur playing with the legendary Dutch Harrison at the 1963 Odessa Pro-Am when Fleckman won with Johnson.

Looking back at his pro career, Fleckman said he played some good golf. He won his first tournament, the Cajun Classic, but never achieved the type of success many thought he would have. "He went (to Byron Nelson) to change his swing and never really got there," Fetters said. "Byron told him everything right but it was a complicated movement."

Even Fleckman admits he probably should have left good enough alone with the swing that enabled him to win a lot as an amateur. "I started a battle between my mind and my heart," Fleckman said at a *First Tee* clinic a couple of years ago in Longview. He went on to tell the young golfers in attendance that he probably shouldn't have done that and just trusted a swing that worked.

Today Fleckman still plays competitively in the senior events around Houston and teaches with Texas Golf Hall of Fame instructor Jim Hardy. Fleckman said:

> *I continue to work on my game and teach a lot. If you want to be a good teacher, you have to continuously learn and continuously work on your own game. I never ask a student to do something that I can't do. I get to sit in on some lessons with Jim and some tour players. So I am continuously learning and competing. I like to compete.*

That being said, it is easy to assume that Fleckman still looks like a Greek god. One who plays senior golf instead of the beer and barbecue circuit.

El Champo in El Campo

"No can do."

Dennis Walters

Fort Lauderdale, Florida

Dennis Walters is now a well-known professional golfer who both entertains and inspires people with his exhibitions of shot making while strapped to a special golf cart. Walters was injured in a golf cart accident in the early 1970s and though paralyzed from the waist down, has fought his way back into golfing prominence through an intense love of the game and tenacious determination. He was the 2008 recipient of PGA of America's Distinguished Service Award.

Before his accident, Walters, a New Jersey native, played college golf at the University of North Texas. With his teammate and still close friend, Guy Cullins of Kerrville, Walters traveled the barbecue circuit.

In his book, *In My Dreams I Walk With You,* Walters recounts his win at an invitational at El Campo. He came to the small town just an hour or so southwest of Houston as a complete stranger. Like other tournaments of that era, El Campo had a nice sized Calcutta pool.

Walters titled the chapter *El Champo of El Campo* and it concludes with the quintessential beer and barbecue scenario.

> *Our group had a gallery of 150 to 200 people, some in golf carts and some just walking with us, when a middle-aged man comes up alongside me as I was climbing up the hill to the elevated 18th tee. He put his arm around my shoulders and said, "Son, do you see those oil wells over there?"*

I told him that I did and he said, "well, I think I can raise a few thousand dollars if you could hit one." I was glad no one else was close enough to hear the guy because the oil wells he was referring to were out of bounds. He was suggesting that I could make more money by intentionally losing the tournament than I could make by winning... No can do, I promptly replied

Walters then striped one down the middle and made an easy par to win. Later he collected his winner's booty and like so many before him, floated down the highway to the next tournament, feeling like the richest man in Texas.

SECTION IV: MISCELLANEOUS

"Well, I'm Miscellaneous now."

Molly Grubb (1967 Miss Texas)
Tyler, Texas

Money

Calcutta money is a funny thing to talk about. Some guys are loose about it, figuring it is always best to just tell the truth and hope that the statute of limitations may have run its course. Others are reticent, a little embarrassed by a reality of years gone by and still others will just deny it or act like it never happened.

According to one former player with a good college golfing record, it was just the way that kids were able to pay for their golf during the summer months. In a large sense, for the golfers, it wasn't gambling at all but just receiving a gift from a grateful gambler. The exception is the golfer who buys part of his action and has some skin in the game, which some did, usually with disastrous results.

But others learned they could handle such pressure and made money beyond their comprehension as young men who had never really been in the job market at that point. They were just playing golf and having fun. And the people in the towns wanted the best younger players to come to their town and their little golf course to see how they might match up against the local legend.

Palestine was especially that way with the Silver Fox, Leroy Roquemore. If a guy like John Mahaffey beat Roquemore at Palestine, he knew he had really done something. Indicative of the local merchants supporting the event was the starter at Palestine, Emmitt Pryor, who owned a men's clothing store in town. He was a mainstay as the starter at the first tee and since the Palestine tournament was always the Fourth of July weekend,

Pryor often got a pretty young woman to model a patriotic red, white and blue bikini while assisting him in his starter duties.

There is even one case of a golfer playing poorly but still receiving a gift from the people he stayed with during the tournament and that, quite frankly, is extraordinary and captures the spirit of the beer and barbecue circuit—local people loved their tournaments and it was something they looked forward to each year.

Just to be fair to those who were willing to share their experiences with Calcutta money, the names attached to the following remarks have been omitted. Here is a collection of remarks about "funny money."

> *Of course when we were still in college, we could get in trouble if we took any money so I would put it in the back of my trunk.*

> *I played at Center one time and stayed with a very nice older couple. He was the small town doctor and when I was ready to leave, he said that he and his wife wanted me to take a girl to dinner when I got back to school. I drank too much and may not have broken 80 the whole tournament but there was more than $100 in the envelope which was a lot of money in the early 1970s.*

> *Back then, there were rules of conduct and what have you, but it kind of went out of the window or something. I remember going to an NCAA tournament and they were saying all of these things that you couldn't do and we were sitting there going, "if this is really true and enforced, then the only team that would be here would be Harvard."*

> *I was playing in the national amateur and lost my first match so I called to see if they would let me in the tournament and they did. So I called a friend and said I am playing good and let's go over there tomorrow night and buy me. That was the 50th year of the tournament and I tied for first and got beat in a playoff.*

> *I'll tell you a good Calcutta story. There was a guy here who bought a guy for $1,000 and had to play him in the first round. He had to beat a guy he bought in the Calcutta and did.*

> *I remember getting $1,400 from the Calcutta and felt like a rich man.*

I had half of myself for about $750 and won the tournament. A couple of guys sold for almost 10 grand each so it was a nice little take.

He gave me a grand so I guess he made $10,000. All I know is that I called into work the next day and said I was done for the summer.

He gave me a check and I sweated it pretty good. I was about half way home when I had to take a look. I saw a three and just kept looking and it was $300! I felt on top of the world because I needed the money then.

He was the last guy to sell. His friend was the hotshot that everyone wanted to buy and I asked him if he ever beat his friend and he said about half the time. Right then, I knew I was going to buy him. Well, some guy in the back keeps out bidding me. I went back there and it was my friend Ron so I told him I am going to buy him so why don't we just go into together. We did and he wins the tournament. We win about twenty grand. We paid about $800 for him.

You never went to anybody and asked, "what's my cut if I play good and make you some money?" That just wasn't done. But it was kind of assumed that if you placed first or second and they made some money, then they would give you a few dollars.

Center was a great tournament. I played in it my second year of college and won it. I don't remember any money. I guess I got cheated out of my money. I just remember winning the trophy.

"Did you win a nice trophy?" my mom asked. "No," I said, "I won $3,100."

Ahead of Their Time

"I'm proud to have helped kids learn the game and appreciate its traditions."

Dudley Wysong

McKinney, Texas

Like many of the top players on the beer and barbecue circuit, two standouts from the North Texas area went on to have good professional careers. And they were known among their peers as great players. But more than their playing achievements, these two men, one living and one deceased, found more lasting satisfaction in helping underprivileged kids learn the game of golf.

In the golf world's parlance, these two men are distinguished for "giving back to the game."

The first man died before his time due to an unusual heart condition. He grew up privileged, the son of a doctor in McKinney, but found his greatest joy later in life among the poor. He devoted much of his time teaching kids, who would normally never have the chance, how to play golf.

The second man still lives and works in Fort Worth where he learned the game and first excelled in competition. He did well as a junior, then in college, and for a while on the PGA Tour. He would much rather talk about the *First Tee* program in his hometown than about winning the Center Invitational, which he did twice in the late 1970s. The first man also won at Center and other stops along the way such as Tyler's Briarwood Invitational.

With the advent of the *First Tee* program to help kids learn the game of golf and how its principles can be helpful in life, it seems appropriate to recognize these two men who were truly ahead of their time in seeing the need. Before the *First Tee* was ever conceived in its present state, Dudley Wysong of McKinney and Lindy Miller of Fort Worth were making a difference in the lives of underprivileged children in their communities.

Wysong started a program through the McKinney YMCA in the 1980s when he was the pro at McKinney Country Club. But before his days of helping kids he had a long and successful playing career as both an amateur and a professional.

When golfers of the stature of Miller Barber and Jacky Cupit say you can play, it is a safe bet that you have some game. Both men saw up close the good play of Dudley Wysong. Barber lost to Wysong in what Billy Bob Thomason of Center calls the best match he ever saw in the first Center Invitational in 1958 while Cupit just says that Wysong was a fine player who belongs in the Texas Golf Hall of Fame.

"The best I recall, Barber hit every green in regulation and still lost," Thomason said. "Wysong was running in putts from everywhere. I was playing somebody but more caught up in watching that match of two great players."

Wysong did not win that year at Center, losing instead to Thomason the next day.

"He fired so many bullets at Barber that he just wasn't himself in our match," Thomason said. "We played early that next morning and he just wasn't himself."

Thomason in turn lost to the first winner of the Center Invitational, M.H. Hopson of Jacksonville, a high school coach and father of Mike Hopson, who also won a lot of barbecue tournaments. The first year was the only year that Center used match play so Wysong simply returned the next year and won in a medal play format.

He also won the Briarwood Invitational in 1962 over a great field that featured Homero Blancas as the defending champion. Wysong was a man who practiced a lot and grooved a pretty swing. "I remember watching him practice back then," T.C. Hamilton said. "And he just hit every shot so solidly. He would hit a lot of balls and just have this trench dug out where he was hitting those solid iron shots. He was a terrific player."

Wysong's amateur career included a finals match against the great Jack Nicklaus at Pebble Beach in 1961. He lost the match, 8 and 6, but did not let that experience derail his golfing ambitions. He later turned professional and won twice on the PGA Tour, first at the Phoenix Open in 1966 and again in 1967 at the Hawaiian Open. He finished second to Al Geiberger in the 1966 PGA Championship.

Born and raised in McKinney, Wysong was introduced to golf at an early age by his father who was a medical doctor and a friend of Byron

Nelson. The McKinney medical clinic is still named after the senior Wysong. Suffering from a rare aneurism near his heart, Wysong died at the young age of 58 at the McKinney Country Club where he served as the head pro.

Miller formed his own golf foundation while serving as the head golf professional at Mira Vista Country Club on the Southwest side of Fort Worth in the early 1990s. A world beater from early on, he won the Fort Worth city junior in 1973 before embarking on an outstanding college career at Oklahoma State. While on a college team with future touring pros Bob Tway and David Edwards, Miller was an All-America selection all four years. The Cowboys won the NCAA title twice with Miller leading the way.

Miller's amateur record was superb. He tied for 16th in the 1978 Masters won by Gary Player. His two-under par 286 was the lowest amateur total at Augusta since 1961, when Charlie Coe of Oklahoma City finished in a tie for second in another Masters won by Player.

Of his two wins at Center, Miller was once the recipient of a gift from Billy Pierot of Athens. It was in 1978 and Pierot just had a tap-in putt on his last hole to win the tournament outright. He missed and in the subsequent playoff, Miller won. He thus became the only player to win back-to-back titles at a barbecue tournament known for its outstanding fields. Later, after the college players quit coming to Center, others won consecutive times but Miller's two wins remain a significant accomplishment. He also won the Southern Amateur and Pacific Coast Amateur before turning pro in 1978.

His pro career was good but not what some might have expected. He never won on the PGA Tour but did claim a win on the Nationwide Tour.

Once Miller retired from touring golf, he became pro at Mira Vista and started his foundation. It became a blueprint, of sorts, for the *First Tee* that was founded in 1997. The *First Tee* now has a well advertised goal of reaching 10 million children for its programs.

Charles Cline of the Fort Worth *Star Telegram*, wrote about Miller's foundation in September of 1997.

While Tiger Woods provides the inspiration, Lindy Miller is providing the means.

Woods, of multiracial heritage, has been credited with causing a golfing boom, especially among children and minorities, after his stunning success as an amateur and on the PGA Tour. But inspiration can't buy lessons, clubs, golf balls, or pay green fees.

That's why the Lindy Miller Foundation for Junior Golf could become a model for similar programs around the nation. In the foundation's first summer alone, approximately 60 needy youngsters of all races participated in free golf programs at five Fort Worth community centers. For many, it was their first contact with the sport.

More than just provide a free clinic for the youngsters, Miller pushed for a more comprehensive program that would also teach life skills. He raised money and heightened community awareness of the need to make golf accessible on a regular basis for children who normally could not afford to participate. He made a difference and now it is safe to say that the *First Tee* did use some of Miller's foresight in establishing its programs.

And like a proud father, Miller was in attendance in December of 2011 when the Ben Hogan Learning Center was opened at the *First Tee* at Rockwood Golf Course in Fort Worth.

Wysong's approach was similar even though more modest, but his ideas were promoted some ten years before Miller. In an article written by Curt Sampson in *Texas Golf Legends*, Wysong has this to say of his legacy in golf.

I started a program with McKinney YMCA to expose kids to golf—to tell them where it came from, how it started. I go out every afternoon (in the summer) to teach 10 or 15 kids at the McKinney Municipal. The great thing is getting poor kids out on the golf course. I'm proud to have helped kids learn the game and appreciate its traditions.

Well done Mr. Wysong. Well done Mr. Miller.

Chip Shots

"I am the man!"

Rocky Thompson

Plano, Texas

A lot of the old time sportswriters had a weekly column about tidbits from the world of sports that did not constitute a story. The items were always brief, pithy and informative. This is a similar assortment from the beer and barbecue circuit that is built on interesting statements.

And I bogeyed the last hole. They had the fairway trap shaved on the left side so that the ball funneled into it and that's exactly where my ball ended up. I could only barely blast out and take my chances to make a hard par.

This is from Mark Hayes, recalling his still record 18-hole score of 63 at the 1977 British Open at Turnberry. The record has been tied several times but never broken. Hayes won on the beer and barbecue circuit (the 1969 Briarwood Invitational) while a standout at Oklahoma State University in the late 1960 and early 1970s. He was also a junior phenom from Oklahoma, winning the Texas Oklahoma junior. He won the Byron Nelson in 1976 and The Players Championship in 1977.

I've played in over a thousand golf tournaments.

This one is from Rocky Thompson, the irrepressible mayor of Toco, Texas, on the putting green after the second round of the 1989 Bellsouth Classic in Atlanta. This was when the red-headed journeyman was on the cusp of joining the Champions Tour. He explained that he played in something every weekend whether it was on tour or at some small town on the barbecue circuit.

I am the man!

This was shouted from the top his lungs by the same irrepressible mayor of Toco when he won his first tournament on either tour, the MONY Syracuse Senior Classic in 1991. Thompson went on to win again in 1991 and had a third win in 1994.

Daddy and I qualified and made the cut in the 1966 PGA Team Championship.

This one is from John Lively, Jr., the oldest of the two sons of John Lively, a longtime golf professional in East Texas. It was the elder Lively who bought Charles Coody in the Calcutta at Willow Brook in Tyler in 1960 and with his winnings helped Coody make his way to the U.S. Open at Cherry Hills in Denver. It was highly unusual for a father/son duo to play in a PGA Tour partnership in those days. John, Jr. and his brother Billy own the Tawakoni Golf Club and were recently honored by the Northern Texas PGA for their lifetime contributions to golf. Both of the Lively brothers played the tour during the late 1960s and early 1970s and won their share of beer and barbecue tournaments, especially in the Athens area in the late 1950s and early 1960s.

You know, Orville Moody played in this thing several years ago. Can you imagine a U.S. Open champion playing in this deal?

From a fellow competitor in the 27 holes in a one day Yamboree two person scramble at the nine-hole Gilmer Country Club. My brother Tim and I both looked at each other and said, "Wow." Old Sarge just loved to play and could definitely golf his ball. He lived quietly in the Sulphur Springs area of East Texas after his years on the senior tour were done. He was the last man to win the U.S. Open after going through both local and sectional qualifying and it will probably be a long time before someone does it again. He passed away in 2008 but after a Champions Tour record of 11 wins that included the U.S. Senior Open. Moody will always be in the elite company of men to have won both the U.S. Open and the U.S. Senior Open: Arnold Palmer, Jack Nicklaus, Gary Player, Lee Trevino, and Hale Irwin.

The Greatest Beer and Barbecue Tournament of All

"Do you know the biggest beer and barbecue tournament of all time? It's the Masters."

Andy Dillard

Oklahoma City, Okla.

There is simply no other tournament in the world like The Masters. It is the only one of the four majors that returns to the same venue each year and has a flavor that is truly unique.

For the golfing world to annually converge on the town of Augusta, Georgia each year is like Tyler or Longview hosting a World Series or something. Augusta is a nice city of some 100,000 but it lacks the infrastructure for such an enormous event. To understand the magnitude of the tournament, the La Quinta Inn of Augusta was asking $49 a night on the Saturday a week after the tournament. During the tournament, the rooms were $399 per night with a two-night minimum. A friend rented her home for $4,000 that week and the house is about 10 miles from the course.

It wasn't always this way. Another friend's father used to buy 8 or 10 tickets a year in the 1960s as The Masters begged him to help them out. Later he was cut back to four, maximum, and those would be gone when he and his wife passed away. Too bad for his children, they had better get on the waiting list and bide their time.

But The Masters has always had that marketing genius that turns a track meet into the Olympics or a boxing match into an *undisputed World Championship*. Give the guys credit, from Clifford Roberts and Bobby

Jones on down to Billy Payne today, the members of Augusta National Golf Club know how to create and preserve tradition. The tournament and its history are deeply appreciated by those who love golf.

After collecting just about every conceivable logoed item available, an idea was hatched in 2011 to peruse the *pirate lots* along Washington Boulevard that I remembered from the late 1980's when I first made the pilgrimage to Augusta. Back then you could buy a gaudy knock-off that I thought would be good for some fun these days. Forget about it. There is not one soul in Augusta who would dare to sell any faux Masters merchandise for fear of being arrested The golf club runs an advertisement in the local paper the week or two prior to the tournament to warn anyone who might be ignorant of the penalties of selling knock-off merchandise. The club has trademarked the logo and they mean business.

And that in essence is the big difference today. The Masters, like the game of golf, is business. But in the beginning, The Masters was much like the little barbecue tournament in Center, Texas, and everybody had a darn good time. They had a Calcutta and they had parties and Don Cherry even performed one year at a strip tease club, which didn't sit well with Mr. Roberts. But Jones got a laugh out of it for he was not the formal stiff that many might think. In fact, in his final days, he loved to go to Lake Sinclair near Atlanta to play cards with his fishing buddies. They never wet a hook and one of the most endearing pictures of Jones is in a floppy fishing hat with a sly smile just days before his death.

To get a sense of the tournament's early days, a good source of information comes from Gene Sarazen, who won all four modern major championships during a career that spanned 30 years. That achievement puts him in the same company as Ben Hogan, Gary Player, Jack Nicklaus, and Tiger Woods.

Sarazen's era began in the early 1920s against such competition as Walter Hagen and Bobby Jones. For different reasons, he admired both men–Hagen the competitor and Jones the gentleman. Like many of the pros of his time, Sarazen held club pro jobs and made wise investments to make enough money to pursue competitive golf. The purses in those days were tiny but the pros often mingled with men of Jones' stature and thus were privy to good business deals.

In his book, *Thirty Years of Championship Golf*, Sarazen said that he regretted having to miss the inaugural Masters tournament in 1934 because of a prior commitment for a series of exhibition matches in South America. Tall and lanky Horton Smith won that first Masters but Sarazen, was at the top of his game.

So when the second playing of what was then known at the Augusta National Invitation rolled around in 1935, Sarazen was eager to play and arrived a week early for practice rounds. He not only admired Jones but counted him as a dear friend and enjoyed his company. Jones, said Sarazen, always epitomized the best in golf.

Jones had retired from competitive golf after his history-making year in 1930 when he won all four majors at that time–the U.S. Amateur and Open and the British Amateur and Open. But Augusta National co-founder Clifford Roberts prevailed upon Jones to play in the Masters and Jones reluctantly agreed. Roberts rightly knew that Jones' presence was needed to attract the top players and that gate receipts also depended on his participation as a player.

In the first tournament in 1934, Jones finished 13th, 10 shots worse than winner Horton Smith. Jones played in the tournament each year it was contested through 1948 but never bettered that 13th place finish.

Sarazen writes about his first visit in 1935:

> *I was anxious to make a creditable showing in my first Masters, for a representative group of champions, the old and the new, had been invited, and the old master himself was competing. The experts didn't think that Bob could win. He had been away from tournament golf for over four years, and that's too long a time for even the greatest of golfers. Jones went for the highest price in the Calcutta betting pool, with Craig Wood and myself also installed as favorites on the basis of the form we had shown tuning up.*

Bobby Jones selling for the highest amount in the Calcutta did not seem logical but gambling seldom is stimulated by sound thinking. More often, it is influenced by the buyer's fondness for a certain player or to show others that he has enough money to do what he wants. The titans of American industry were no doubt involved in those early Calcutta pools at Augusta. There probably wasn't a trace of shadiness among the genteel crowd. So what if Jones hadn't played competitively in years, by God, I am going to buy him and your man is going to have to beat him to prove me wrong.

According to many in the heyday of the beer and barbecue circuit just after World War II, the same was true with a Dallas car dealer and Earl Stewart, Jr. This man would even buy Stewart when a victory wouldn't return a large enough percentage to cover his purchase price. Money wasn't the real object as much as showing a faith in "my man" and his ability to beat "your man." Of course, winning a little was even better because these same titans didn't accumulate wealth by letting their egos overrun their business instincts. It's just that golf and gambling were a recreation and entertainment in an era before Vegas and other distractions.

There is a picture of the Masters field in 1935 that shows lots of Texans in attendance. There is Byron Nelson, of course, and Ben Hogan and Ralph Guldahl, well known pros early in their careers.

Also in the field in 1935 were Dallas amateurs Gus Moreland and Jack Munger as well as a young man from Louisville, Kentucky, Wilford Wehrle, who would later play at the Premier Invitational in Longview in 1948 and lose to Earl Stewart, Jr. in the finals.

In the late 1940s and then into the 1950s, another darling amateur of the Masters was Charlie Coe of Oklahoma City. He played the beer and barbecue circuit in Texas and Oklahoma and is listed on the Premier Invitational Calcutta board with other fine amateurs of his day such as 1951 U.S. Amateur champion Billy Maxwell of Abilene.

Ben Crenshaw is a golf historian who also won a couple of green jackets at The Masters in 1984 and 1995. He made the following observations about the gambling that was so prevalent during the 1930s and 1940s.

It is said that Bobby Cruikshank placed a bet that Jones would win the Grand Slam in 1930 when he was back in England. He made enough money with that wager to basically comfortably retire... And one of the main reasons that Jones retired when he did was because of the pressure he always felt because his friends had money and were betting such big amounts on him each time he played.

While an admirer of Jones, Sarazen was not overly impressed with Augusta National at first sight. He said he was "let down" on his first visit because the course had several weak holes, most especially the 10th and the 16th. Sarazen does go on to say that Jones should be commended for asking for honest criticism, which Sarazen was not shy to give, to be used later to improve the course. Jones later brought in Perry Maxwell and Robert Trent Jones and they helped improve the two holes that Sarazen singled out as weak. The process of always tweaking Augusta National is a policy still practiced today and for the most part applauded by the top players.

As for his performance that first Masters, Sarazen certainly did not disappoint and will be forever remembered for his charge at the end of regulation play. His heroics were brought to mind recently when Louis Oosthuizen made a double eagle at the par-five second hole in the final round of the 2012 tournament.

Needing to play the final four holes in three under, Sarazen, as if on cue, holed a four-wood shot on the par-five 15th, the double eagle heard around the world. Thus he got his three under with one shot and made pars on the final three holes to force Wood into a 36-hole playoff the next day. It was the only time a 36-hole playoff decided the Masters champion and Sarazen easily prevailed.

Then in the late 1950s and early 1960s, The Masters really took off with the beginning of television broadcasts and the emergence of Arnold Palmer as perhaps the most popular player to ever walk the fairways in Augusta. Palmer was a blue-collar version of Jones, a handsome guy who instead of a smooth swing attacked the ball with a vengeance. His charges were trademarked early on and *Arnie's Army* a reliable gallery at every event. The pride of Latrobe, Pennsylvania won titles in even years 1958, 1960, 1962, and 1964.

Now at age 82, he serves as an honorary starter along with Jack Nicklaus and Gary Player. Both Nicklaus and Player won at Augusta in the 1960s and became golf's *Big Three* as the sport became even more popular in America.

A couple of years ago, at the Greenbrier resort in West Virginia, Palmer recounted his start in professional golf and cited a good showing in a Calcutta as springboard. Palmer said of The Greenbrier:

> *I got my start here. It was 1955, my freshman year on the tour, and I couldn't earn money for the first six months.* (An odd rule then when the tour was still part of the PGA of America.) *I was in an apprentice program… But Sam Snead had a tournament here where I could win* (some money) *and he called and invited me to play. That alone was a huge honor* (to be invited by Snead)*… I played in the Pro-Am and in the Calcutta, which we had in those days. I played very well, made a lot of money. And me and my partner Spence Owen made some more money in the Calcutta. So, really, that was my start, that gave me everything I needed to really get my career started.*

Palmer was joined by Nicklaus and Player on the first tee in 2012 to hit the ceremonial first shots of the tournament. It was the first time the *Big Three* had done the honor and hopefully it will not be the last. Hitting those opening shots is another tradition preserved by the Augusta National as it continues to embrace golf history.

Player was the last to hit and after his shot, Masters chairman Billy Payne confirmed that the Masters is one high flying beer and barbecue tournament. He loudly proclaimed to those assembled near the first tee: "The 2012 Masters is now underway. Have fun!"

The Calcutta Finale

"I got involved on a preventive basis."

Duke Butler

Ponte Vedra Beach, Florida

It was a typical warm and humid June night in deep East Texas when the Chevy flatbed truck rolled up to its usual place beneath the pine trees. Adorned with Christmas lights that sparkled against the water of the small lake near the ninth green, the atmosphere was just perfect for a rollicking night of good fun.

The beer had been flowing all day at Center Country Club and the chickens were just about ready. The huge barbecue grills down near the pond were churning out the yard birds like nobody's business. This was going to be some party tonight. The patrons were ready to PARTAY!

Starting early that morning, the men who cook the chickens were sampling the beer as much as the players and those who had come out to watch the qualifying rounds. The top amateur golfers not just in East Texas or even Texas, but in the entire country, were out on the nine-hole links. The barbecue chicken would be delicious as it had been each year since the first Center Invitational in 1958.

There is no telling how many barbecued chickens would be served that night to a festive crowd but no one would leave hungry. Center is poultry country, pure and simple. A lot of chicken is raised in Shelby County and the surrounding area and since Americans were now told to be healthier by eating less beef, the farmers were doing just fine financially, thank you very much.

Some of those farmers, and their wives, would be bringing some of that chicken money to the Calcutta. The wives usually had their own little syndicates and would get together for lunch or for tea or just about any other reason to discuss who they should buy at the Calcutta.

One group of ladies hit the jackpot in 1979 so optimism was still high that they could do it again. Come to think of it, optimism is always a big part of gambling—optimism and ego. This is especially so for the men with some buyers taking a good player at a high cost just to share in the limelight on Sunday evening when the cash is doled out to the winners.

A crowd of young and handsome golfers and their lady friends mingled in the spotlight that evening. A lot of the college golfers didn't have dates but that would not be a problem. "College girls from all over East Texas would come to the tournament and especially the Calcutta," a local Center businessman said. "We had cars parked on both sides of Highway 96 for what looked like miles."

As expected, some of the golfers drank a little too much beer and that would be a problem. A couple of big name golfers in the past had played miserably their first time at the Center Invitational simply because they had too much fun. Those same players came back a second time and redeemed themselves by winning the tournament.

But it was the older folks with deep pockets who would make things interesting that night. A lot of the older folks were in their sharpest duds and held glasses of bourbon or scotch to sip while contemplating their chances to make some big money. Most were already wealthy so winning was really secondary to having some fun.

The sheriff of Shelby County was on hand to greet folks. Although gambling might be illegal, technically speaking, the invitational golf tournament in Center was the biggest social event of the year and no one wanted to put a damper on the festivities. The tournament was an established institution by 1982. Many of the past champions had gone on to greatness on the PGA Tour so the tournament was a showcase of future golf stars.

The syndicate of women had hit the jackpot just three years earlier in 1979 when blond haired Kevin Harrison of Oklahoma State University took home the top prize. Sometimes the ladies picked the most handsome college golfer and sometimes they stayed with the facts. Most of all, they had to stay within their budget or at least close to it. The field for the tournament was especially strong this year with four of the top five finishers in the NCAA tournament on hand.

There was also a buzz about the size of the Calcutta. Although it was big each year, the total had never gone over $100,000 but some thought this might be the year.

Practice rounds were in full swing and the field was so impressive with Billy Ray Brown of the University of Houston the main attraction. Tall, sturdy, and handsome, Brown had just won the NCAA individual title at Pinehurst in North Carolina with a third round 65 on the difficult number two course. The runner-up that year, Andy Dillard of Oklahoma State was also in the field. A native of Tyler, just 80 miles north and west of Center, Dillard was already a well known player at Center.

Another top finisher from the NCAA tournament held just the week before were Danny Briggs of Texas A&M and Paris, Texas, a town near the Oklahoma border in East Texas. Briggs, like Dillard, was known not only for good golf but for good times.

John Slaughter and Mark Fuller were teammates of Brown's at the University of Houston and both finished in the top five at the NCAA.

A look back at the previous winners of the Center tournament showed six players who would later win on the PGA Tour and two would win majors. Ben Crenshaw won in 1973 and then went on to win the Masters twice and John Mahaffey who also won, took home the PGA Championship at Oakmont in Pennsylvania in 1978.

Other winners to later claim tour wins were Dudley Wysong of McKinney, Texas in 1959, Jackie Cupit of Longview in 1960, Homero Blancas of Houston in 1964, Marty Fleckman of Port Arthur in 1965, Bruce Lietzke of Beaumont in 1972, and Keith Fergus of Killeen in 1974.

The list of non-winners who played at Center is equally impressive. Bob Tway of Marietta, Georgia, and Hal Sutton of Shreveport both played and did not win but later won the PGA Championship. Center was known in the golfing world for being a fun tournament with a great field.

Local Center businessman Billy Bob Thomason said:

And it was known far and wide for a big Calcutta. I remember playing in a pro-am in Vegas one time with Jay Delsing. And he is from Illinois or someplace and as we are walking down the first fairway making our introductions, I said I was from Center, Texas, and Delsing didn't miss a beat and said to me, "the town with the big Calcutta."

The big Calcutta in 1982 was about to begin. As the sun began to go down, the last qualifying rounds were turned in and the crowd gathered down by the lake. There was definitely a buzz in the air. Right on cue, the flatbed truck carrying the three auctioneers made its way down the hill to the area where 300 people sat enjoying their drinks and barbecue. By now, all of the golfers and the pretty young college girls were on hand for a good party.

Brown had already met a beauty and was enjoying himself immensely. After the truck was stationed and the loud speakers checked, the auctioneer wasted little time starting the Calcutta. His enthusiasm was over the top:

Ladies and gentlemen, welcome to the 1982 Center Invitational, and we have some of the best amateurs in the country here tonight. I am talking about some future PGA Tour stars ladies and gentlemen. So don't be shy. You know golf and you know your golfers so make some money tonight!

We are going to start with Billy Ray Brown. This boy can flat out play. He just finished his freshman year at the University of Houston and just won the NCAAs. You heard me right, ladies and gentlemen, a freshman and won the NCAAs. He just got here from North Carolina. He won at Pinehurst #2 and it is one of the great courses in this country.

Dillard remembers the moment well. "The auctioneer said we are going to sell the NCAA champion Billy Ray Brown first and who'll give me $2,000? Someone yelled out, I'll give you $10 thousand!"

"After a moment of stunned silence," Dillard said. "Everyone said holy crap!"

Speechless for the first time in his life, the auctioneer, nicknamed *Squirrelly*, finally blurted out, "You just bought yourself an NCAA champion."

The game was definitely on. The buzz was even more intense. This was going to be some Calcutta. "It was a wild night with a lot of drinking," Dillard said. "About half way through the evening, the siren in the sheriff's car goes off. Someone had gotten in it and flipped on the siren."

With a start like that, it is no wonder the total pool grew throughout the evening and went over $100,000 for the first time.

At some point during the proceeding, a local attorney bought a young unknown player from Oklahoma, Clay Simmons, for a song. He went on the win the tournament and his payout was north of $40,000. The rumor was that he was last seen headed back north of the Red River with a Footjoy shoebox full of cash.

But the fallout from that evening was just beginning. Brown did not have a good tournament and like many before him, was probably a victim of too much wine and song. Mahaffey was a victim of the same his first trip to Center in 1968. He was found one morning asleep on the doorstep of the clubhouse. He didn't do well that year but returned the next year and won the tournament.

So Brown's disappointing performance was not unusual. The same could be said of Crenshaw, who first played in 1972 but did not do well. He came back and won in 1973 and had to do so for his buyer to make any money because, like Brown, he had gone for a very high price in the Calcutta. Brown returned to Houston while the PGA Tour was in California for the U.S. Open that would be won with Tom Watson's famous chip-in on the 17th hole.

Dillard said:

> The next week at the U.S. Open at Pebble, Crenshaw and some others were asking Willie Wood about the Calcutta. Word got back to the USGA. Duke Butler asked Billy Ray about it and the next thing you knew, the Ohio State coach had called the NCAA and three of us had to write letters to keep our eligibility. I didn't take any money because my dad always handled that. So I said in the letter that I took no money. I was cleared and so were Willie and Tommy... Thing is, the Ohio State players had played in a Calcutta tournament in Kalimazoo, Michigan, the same week. At least, that is what I heard.

Dillard played in beer and barbecue tournaments for years during the 1970s and 1980s and explained the appeal of those tournaments in a bygone era.

> I played in my first barbecue tournament when I was 13 at Briarwood in Tyler. I played at Center a lot as both a collegian and a pro. You knew what you were there for, to play for the money... A lot of kids today, they wouldn't understand it but back then there weren't a lot of tournaments around. Playing for money is different than playing for trophies. The real pressure is when you are playing for your own money so I never liked to have any of myself in a Calcutta.

That wasn't the case for Tom Evans of Dallas in the 1974 Center Invitational. A seasoned player from Dallas and LSU, Evans came to Center with some of the Tenison Park gang and it was suggested that he had a big part of the action. The pressure of that or from just leading the tournament seemed to get to him as he missed short putts on the last two holes to let Fergus take home the top prize.

But the Calcutta got just a little too big in 1982. Once the college players realized they could lose their eligibility, the risk was too great to play at Center or the other tournaments.

"I was concerned about the top players at the University of Houston going there (Center) and making money," Butler said. "I was trying to protect the amateur status of the top players. I was worried someone else would get involved so I got involved on a preventive basis... I was concerned about the Billy Ray Browns of the world, quite frankly."

Butler's efforts reached the desk of one P.J. Boatwright, the executive director of the USGA. Hard to believe, but a Calcutta in a tiny town in deep East Texas was the topic of much conversation at the Golf House in Far Hills, New Jersey. Of course P.J., in spite of his much esteemed status as the head of the USGA, was also a deep lover of golf and knew a thing or two about Calcutta betting. He listed a win over Harvie Ward at the Biltmore Invitational as one of the highlights of his amateur career and you can bet there was betting there, no pun intended. Boatwright is even on a Calcutta sheet displayed at the venerable Palmetto Golf Club in Aiken, South Carolina, just across the Savannah River from the folks at Augusta National. Matter of fact, Boatwright was the highest seller in that particular Calcutta in 1953.

Considering his knowledge of barbecue tournaments, Boatwright was somewhat lenient in that the letter allowed the top finishers to remain amateurs if they received no money or returned it. The USGA rulebook now states that just participation in a Calcutta event can put a player's amateur status at risk.

"I don't know how influential my remarks were but I was concerned about it because it might affect their amateur status and college eligibility," Butler said. "I'm a little fuzzy about it but Mr. P.J. Boatwright was one of the most respected gentlemen in the history of the game."

Sadly, Boatwright succumbed to cancer in the late 1980s when he was just 61 years old. He was an innovative administrator and now an internship with the USGA is named is his honor. P.J., in another set of circumstances, probably in his college days, would have enjoyed the fun and competition in Center.

Now a PGA Tour consultant, Butler's intentions were noble. And Brown is now a well known and well paid television announcer.

But it signaled the end of an era. An era that was boundless in its stories of great golf and great fun. An era that began shortly after America had prevailed in World War II.

Epilogue

The bleak scenery is startling. A fence with no trespassing signs prohibits a closer look but I make out the giant oak tree near the putting green. What was once vibrant is now dead and casting a spooky silhouette against an autumn sky.

Weeds and abandoned golf carts dominate the landscape. The windows of the simple clubhouse are shattered or boarded up.

This was my field of dreams.

Sipping coffee, I let my mind go back to a time when Bellwood Golf Club was filled with golfers. Never a country club, Bellwood was a public course for working people with unbridled personalities. Their commonality was a love for golf and not much else.

Over there is Wiltzie Hail scavenging along the weeds of the railroad tracks for golf balls. On the putting green is Frank Dunn, a tall and awkwardly supple left-handed golfer who could really play. But he was no match for Buford Rose, whose patented shot with a driver was a hook fade. Don't ask me how, but many times I saw Rose let it fly off the first tee and the ball would begin to draw before drifting back to right and finding the center of the fairway–a hook fade.

To the left is what is left of the 9th green. It is now covered with waist-high weeds but once had a small drop off to the right that always left you a pop-up pitch shot that we called a cut shot. It is now termed a flop shot but L.V. Scott (Scotty) taught me how to hit it with my old McGregor dual wedge that had a split sole. Oh how I loved to practice that shot.

My stare rivets to the first tee. Oh my, there is my dad and his regular group on a Saturday morning. There is Bill Pace taking one of his too many practice swings and a huge divot hits my dad in the back of his neck. An impressive string of expletives follows. He is both admonished and comforted by Lowry Jones, the octogenarian who couldn't carry his drive more than 120 yards but could hit it through a small doorway. He had his own rickety golf cart without a top and routinely went around Bellwood in the low 70s. Did I mention that he could putt! Or that the course was about 5,600 yards from the tips.

Wow, there is Max Byrd, who couldn't play a lick but dressed better than Doug Sanders. He once missed our driveway with all four wheels when driving my dad home one evening. My mother made him drink lots of coffee at our kitchen table before letting him drive home. And I can't leave out Forest Byous – that's B-Y-O-U-S.

These men not only played golf together every Saturday, they loved each other. These men showed our family how much they cared when we suffered some hard times. They are all gone now but not forgotten.

My generation grew up playing golf for the most part unsupervised. We were dropped off at the golf course at 9 am and picked up at dark thirty. We played all day and seldom practiced. We hunted golf balls and consumed large amounts of lemonade during hot Texas summers. Our junior tour was Tyler, Jacksonville, Longview, Kilgore, Canton—the small towns within an hour's drive. Most only had nine holes but featured different sets of tees to make them more interesting.

People always made fun of Bellwood Golf Club because it was the lowest on the totem pole of the three courses in Tyler during the 1960s. But it was my home course. It was where I learned to play a game that I still love intensely.

I remember walking three miles alone as a 9-year-old boy to watch the Briarwood Invitational. I wasn't old enough for Little League. Then as a 6th grader, I invited Mark Triggs to play at Bellwood. He was 12 years old and shot a 73. I couldn't believe my eyes but I was hooked.

I thank the Lord for golf and the people who love the game. I guess a big part of me had to write this book. I hope you enjoyed it.

JPW

Tournament Winners

Briarwood Invitational winners

1958 – A.J. Triggs, Tyler, Texas
1959 – T.C. Hamilton, Tyler, Texas
1960 – Jacky Cupit, Longview, Texas
1961 – Homero Blancas, Houston, Texas
1962 – Dudley Wysong, McKinney, Texas
1963 – Marty Fleckman, Port Arthur, Texas
1964 – Marty Fleckman, Port Arthur, Texas
1965 – A.J. Triggs, Tyler, Texas
1966 – Ras Allen, Denton, Texas
1967 – Jeff Voss, Dallas, Texas
1968 – Arnold Salinas, Dallas, Texas
1969 – Mark Hayes, Stillwater, Oklahoma
1970 – David Montgomery, Dallas, Texas
1971 – Mark Triggs, Tyler, Texas
1972 – David Price, Odessa, Texas
1973 – Mark Triggs, Tyler, Texas
1974 – Elroy Marti, Houston, Texas
1975 – Van Gillen, Conroe, Texas
1976 – Blaine McCallister, Fort Stockton, Texas
1977 – Blaine McCallister, Fort Stockton, Texas
1978 – Jimmy Wheeler, Dallas, Texas
1979 – David Sann, Dallas, Texas
1980 – Mike Neece, Irving, Texas

Premier Invitational Champions

1943 – Johnny Garrison
1944 – Johnny Garrison
1945 – Dick Martin
1946 – Earl Stewart, Jr.
1947 – Earl Stewart, Jr.
1948 – Palmer Lawrence
1949 – Joe Moore

1950 – Dick Martin
1951 – Raleigh Selby
1952 – John Stamner
1953 – J.H. "Doc" Brinkley
1954 – Roane Puett
1955 – Bobby Vickers
1956 – H. P. Childress
1957 – Bus Atkinson
1958 – Bobby Sharp
1959 – Jacky Cupit
1960 – Jacky Cupit
1961 – Roy Pace
1962 – Homero Blancas

The Firecracker Open Winners

1946 – Dudley Krueger
1947 – Claude Wild, Jr.
1948 – Walter Benson, Jr.
1949 – Claude Wild, Jr.
1950 – Claude Wild, Jr.
1951 – Dudley Krueger
1952 – Bill Gainer
1953 – Jimmie Connolly
1954 – Walter Benson, Jr.
1955 – Chuck Ribelin
1956 – Ernie George
1957 – Billy Penn
1958 – Sonny Rhodes
1959 – Randy Petri
1960 – Ray Kizer
1961 – George McCall
1962 – Randy Petri
1963 – Roane Puett
1964 – Larry Roden
1965 – Randy Petri
1966 – Roane Puett
1967 – Eugene Mitchell
1968 – Tom Kite
1969 – Ben Crenshaw
1970 – Mason Adkins
1971 – Ben Crenshaw
1972 – Blair Douglas
1973 – Mason Adkins

1974 – Mike Allen
1975 – Tim Wilson
1976 – Tim Wilson
1977 – Doug Nelle
1978 – Doug Nelle
1979 – Ralph Cotton
1980 – Doug Nelle
1981 – Brandon Whitman
1982 – Ralph Cotton
1983 – Petey Petri
1984 – Jep Willie
1985 – Ronnie McDougal
1986 – Omar Uresti
1987 – Bill Dodd
1988 – Billy Clagett
1989 – Omar Uresti
1990 – Billy Clagett
1991 – Billy Clagett
1992 – Deron Zinnecker
1993 – Billy Clagett
1994 – Billy Clagett
1995 – Billy Bennett
1996 – Mark McEntire
1997 – Neal Collins
1998 – Mark McEntire
1999 – Matt Dobyns
2000 – Ricky Arzola
2001 – Billy Clagett
2002 – Steven Bright
2003 – Michael Cooper
2004 – Brian Noonan
2005 – Robby Ormand
2006 – Robby Ormand
2007 – Brenden Redfern
2008 – Michael Cooper
2009 – Scott Roudebush
2010 – Stratton Nolen

Center Invitational Winners

1958 – MH Hopson (Jacksonville)
1959 – Dudley Wysong, Jr. (McKinney)
1960 – Jacky Cupit (Longview)
1961 – Mark Hopkins

1962 – Richard Killian
1963—Dick Martin (Dallas)
1964 – Homero Blancas (Houston)
1965 – Marty Fleckman (Port Arthur)
1966 – Lee McDowell (Baytown)
1967 – Mike Mitchell (Texarkana)
1968 – John Mahaffey (Kerrville)
1969 – Bruce Ashworth
1970 – George Machock (Austin)
1971 – Dean Overturf (Dallas)
1972 – Bruce Lietzke (Beaumont)
1973 – Ben Crenshaw (Austin)
1974 – Keith Fergus (Killeen)
1975 – Jamie Gonzales (Rio De Janiero)
1976 – Joe Hager (Dallas)
1977 – Lindy Miller (Fort Worth)
1978 – Lindy Miller
1979 – Kevin Harrison
1980 – Carl Baker (Nacogdoches)
1981 – Eddie Lyons (Shreveport)
1982 – Clay Simmons
1983 – Ben Smith (Dallas)
1984 – Rocky Thompson (Wichita Falls)
1985 – Joe Hager
1986 – John Horne
1987 – Rocky Thompson
1988 – Jeb Stuart
1989 – Greg Hamilton
1990 – Greg Hamilton
1991 – Jeb Stuart
1992 – Joe Whittlesey (Center)
1993 – Eddie Grace
1994 – Eddie Grace
1995 – John Senden (Australia)
1996 – Perry Moss (Shreveport)
1997 – John Riegger (Illinois)
1998 – Andy Dillard (Tyler)
1999 – Andy Dillard
2000 – Mark Walker
2001 – Mark Walker
2002 – Jeb Stuart
2003 – Henry Cagigal (Fort Worth)
2004 – Edward Loar (Rockwall)
2005 – Kevin Dillen
2006 – Jerod Turner

2007 – Michael Connell
2008 – Perry Moss
2009 – Billy Totah
2010 – Mark Walker
2011 – Brian Rowell

Kilgore Meadowbrook Invitational Winners

1937 – Bill Clark (Gladewater)
1938 – Jimmie Gaunt (Longview)
1939 – Bill Clark (Gladewater)
1940 – Billy Russell (Kilgore)
1941 – Raleigh Selby (Kilgore)
1942 – Gerald Joyce (Palestine)
1943 – E.J. Gannon (Dallas)
1944 – Wally Ulrich (Greenville)
1945 – Raleigh Selby (Houston)
1946 – Gerald Joyce (Palestine)
1947 – Earl Stewart, Jr. (Dallas)
1948 – Buster Reed (Dallas)
1949 – Billy Maxwell (Dallas)
1950 – Raleigh Selby (New London)
1951 – Buster Reed (Dallas)
1952 – Benny Castloo (Mineola)
1953 – Leroy Roquemore (Palestine)
1954 – Bobby Cupit (Greggton)
1955 – No tournament
1956 – Jacky Cupit (Greggton)
1957 – Dick Whetzle (Dallas)
1958 – Miller Barber (Texarkana)
1959 – Jacky Cupit (Greggton)
1960 – Gene Teter (Dallas)
1961 – Sam Love (Shreveport)
1962 – Jim Fetters (Port Arthur)
1963 – Roy Pace (Longview)
1964 – Raleigh Selby (Overton)
1965 – Clay Laird (Kilgore)
1966 – Clyde Tomlinson (Longview)
1967 – Earl Clark (Kilgore)
1968 – Jim Murray (Kilgore)
1969 – Clay Laird (Kilgore)
1970 – Clyde Tomlinson (Longview)
1971 – Mike Hopson (Plano)
1972 – Jimmy Stroope (Houston)

1973 – Ernie McCray (Denton)
1974 – Rick Maxey (Longview)
1975 – Rick Maxey (Longview)
1976 – Kenny Rucker (Houston)
1977 – Billy Wiggs (Denton)
1978 – Mike Mayo (Garland)
1979 – Rodney Kimmel (Fox, Oklahoma)
1980 – James Gillentine (Longview)
1981 – Mike Mayo (Garland)
1982 – Ben Smith (Grand Prairie)
1983 – Kevin Dillen (Henderson)
1984 – Mike Tate (Kilgore)
1985 – Angus Baker (Fort Worth)
1986 – Dan Blake (Fort Worth)
1987 – Mike Mayo (Garland)
1988 – David Bowen (Troup)
1989 – Ren Budde (Denton)
1990 – Henry Coffman (Grand Prairie)
1991 – David Cline (College Station)
1992 – Ronnie Hooker (Longview)
1993 – David Bowen (Troup)
1994 – Randy King (Kilgore)
1995 – Randy Smith (Henderson)
1996 – Mark Bradshaw (Magnolia, Arkansas)
1997 – Chris Beall (Jacksonville)
1998 – Seane Richardson (Longview)
1999 – Seane Richardson (Longview)
2000 – Rick Maxey (Longview)
2001 – Jay Mitchell
2002 – Blake Ladd (Sulphur Springs)
2003 – Lance Dunaway (Dallas)
2004 – Blake Ladd (Sulphur Springs)
2005 – Clint Bowden (Gladewater)
2006 – Brent Akins (Spring Hill)
2007 – Reggie Howell (Tyler)
2008 – Rick Maxey (Lake Tyler)
2009 – Joseph Totah (Palestine)
2010 – Blaine Weiterman (Overton)
2011 – Dave Davis (Fort Worth)

Odessa Pro-Am Winners

1949 – Iverson Martin – Jim Simpson
1950 – Byron Nelson – Bo Wininger

1951 – Harry Todd – Don January
1952 – Bo Wininger – Billy Maxwell
1953 – Ray Montgomery – Miller Barber
1954 – Doug Higgins – Ernie Vossler
1955 – Chuck Klein – Ray Hudson
1956 – Ernie Vossler – Rex Baxter
1957 – Jerry Robinson – Miller Barber
1958 – Ernie Vossler – Rex Baxter
1959 – Doug Higgins – Buddy Branum
1960 – Don January – Dick Jennings
1961 – Frank Wharton – John Farguson
1962 – Doug Sanders – Richard Crawford
1963 – Ned Johnson – Marty Fleckman
1964 – Don Massengale – John Farquhar
1965 – Babe Hiskey – Marty Fleckman
1966 – Charles Coody – Richard Patton
1967 – Don Massengale – Rik Massengale
1968 – Don Massengale – Rik Massengale
1969 – Billy Maxwell – Richard Ellis

Abb Roquemore's East Texas Golf Champions

1941 – Palestine – Leonard White (Dallas)
1942 – Palestine – Leonard White
1942 – Kilgore – Gerald Joyce (Palestine)
1945 – Henderson – Leroy Roquemore (Palestine)
1946 – Kilgore – Gerald Joyce
1946 – Lufkin – Jack Laxon (Brownwood)
1946 – Kilgore – Leonard White (Jack Laxon – 2nd)
1946 – Marshall – Jack Laxon
1946 – Gladewater – Jack Laxon
1947 – Palestine – Gerald Joyce (Gene Towry, Dallas – 2nd)
1947 – Lufkin – Bill Philpot (Beaumont)
1947 – Henderson – Johnny Garrison (Tulsa)
1947 – Kilgore – Earl Stewart, Jr. (Dallas) (Gerald Joyce – 2nd)
1948 – Lufkin – F.E. Ames (Beaumont) (Gerald Joyce – 2nd)
1948 – Henderson – Johnny Garrison (Leroy Roquemore – 2nd)
1948 – Nacogdoches – Gerald Joyce (Bob Quattlebaum – 2nd)
1948 – Kilgore – Buster Reed (Dallas) (Gerald Joyce – 2nd)
1948 – Paris – Jack Tinnin (Dallas)
1948 – Marshall – Johnny Garrison
1949 – Nacogdoches – Gerald Joyce (Raleigh Selby, Kilgore – 2nd)
1949 – Henderson – E.F. Crim (Henderson) (Gerald Joyce – 2nd)
1949 – Kilgore – Billy Maxwell (Odessa) (Earl Stewart, Jr., Longview – 2nd)

1949 – Palestine – Gerald Joyce (Raleigh Selby – 2nd)
1950 – Athens – L.M. Crannell (Dallas) (Don Addington, Dallas – 2nd)
1950 – Palestine – Raleigh Selby (Leon Taylor, Tyler – 2nd)
1950 – Palestine – Gerald Joyce (Leroy Roquemore – 2nd)
1951 – Lufkin – Ray Moore (Beaumont) (Leroy Roquemore – 2nd)
1951 – Athens – L.M. Crannell (Marion Hiskey – 2nd)
1951 – Jacksonville – Leroy Roquemore (Don January, Dallas – 2nd)
1951 – Longview Premier – Raleigh Selby (L.M. Crannell – 2nd)
1951 – Palestine – Gerald Joyce
1951 – Trans Mississippi Am – L.M. Crannell
1951 – Nacogdoches – Howie Johnson (Houston)
1952 – Palestine – Raleigh Selby (Bobby Cupit, Dallas – 2nd)
1952 – Nacogdoches – Howie Johnson
1952 – Jacksonville – Terry Morrow
1953 – Southern Amateur – Joe Conrad (San Antonio) (Gay Brewer, Lexington, KY – 2nd)
1953 – Jacksonville – Tommy Cruse (Jacksonville) (Leon Taylor – 2nd)
1953 – Palestine – Raleigh Selby (Gerald Joyce – 2nd)
1953 – Trans Mississippi Am – Joe Conrad
1953 – Nacogdoches – Howie Johnson
1953 – Kilgore – Leroy Roquemore (Joe Conrad – 2nd)
1954 – Palestine – Leroy Roquemore (Bob Bell, Palestine – 2nd)
1954 – Nacogdoches – Howie Johnson (Tommy Cruse – 2nd)
1954 – Tyler Willow Brook – Benny Castloo (Mineola) (Bobby Cupit – 2nd)
1954 – Kilgore – Bobby Cupit (Raleigh Selby – 2nd)
1954 – Trans Mississippi Am – Jim Jackson (Kirkwood, MO) (Rex Baxter, Amarillo – 2nd)
1954 – Jacksonville – John Garrison (Galveston) (Leroy Roquemore – 2nd)
1954 – Marshall – Tommy Cruse (Richard Parvino, Greggton – 2nd)
1954 – Southern Amateur – Joe Conrad
1955 – Crockett – Bob Beall (Palestine) (Bobby Parks, Longview – 2nd)
1955 – Nacogdoches – Gerald Joyce (Rex Baxter – 2nd)
1955 – British Amateur – Joe Conrad
1955 – Palestine – Leroy Roquemore (Jack Black, Palestine – 2nd)
1955 – Jacksonville – Floyd Addington (Dallas)
1956 – Athens – Billy Martindale (Jacksonville) (Jacky Cupit, Greggton – 2nd)
1956 – Jacksonville – Jacky Cupit
1957 – Palestine – Billy Martindale (Gilbert Stubbs, Corsicana – 2nd)
1957 – Lufkin – Leroy Roquemore (Dalton Raiford, Kountz – 2nd)
1957 – Athens – Jacky Cupit (Billy Martindale – 2nd)
1957 – Jacksonville – Richard Dixon (Galveston)
1958 – Henderson – Jacky Cupit (E.F. Crim – 2nd)
1958 – Palestine – Billy Martindale (Frank Wharton, Dallas – 2nd)
1958 – Athens – Billy Martindale (Leroy Roquemore – 2nd)
1958 – Tyler Briarwood – A.J. Triggs (Tyler)

1958 – Jacksonville – Jacky Cupit
1959 – Palestine – Billy Martindale (Gilbert Stubbs – 2nd)
1959 – Tyler Briarwood – T.C. Hamilton (Tyler)
1959 – Jacksonville – Jacky Cupit
1960 – Palestine – Richard Dixon (James Stubbs, Corsicana – 2nd)
1960 – Tyler Briarwood – Jacky Cupit (Chad Hanna, Tyler – 2nd)
1960 – Jacksonville – Jacky Cupit
1961 – Nacogdoches – Leroy Roquemore (Tommy Cruse – 2nd)
1961 – Palestine – Mark Hopkins (Texas City) (Jim Fetters, Port Arthur – 2nd)
1961 – Tyler Briarwood – Homero Blancas (Houston)
1961 – Hot Springs, Ark. – Leroy Roquemore (Tom Stobaugh – 2nd)
1961 – Jacksonville – Tommy Cruse
1962 – Longview Premier -- Homero Blancas (Fred Marti, Baytown – 2nd)
1962—Tyler Briarwood – Dudley Wysong (McKinney)
1963 – Palestine – Leroy Roquemore (Steve Johnson, Tyler – 2nd)
1963 – Tyler Briarwood – Marty Fleckman (Port Arthur)
1963 – Jacksonville – Mark Hopkins
1963 – Athens – Randy Petri (Houston)
1964—Palestine – Wright Garrett (Houston) (Leroy Roquemore – 2nd)
1964 – Trans Mississippi Am – Wright Garrett
1964 – Tyler Briarwood – Marty Fleckman
1965 – Palestine – Leroy Roquemore (Jack Skeen, Tyler – 2nd)
1965 – Jacksonville – Leroy Roquemore (Sandy Haynes, Jacksonville – 2nd)
1965 – Tyler Briarwood – A.J. Triggs (Leroy Roquemore – 2nd)
1966 – Palestine – Leroy Roquemore (George Rives, Jacksonville – 2nd)
1966 – Jacksonville – Leroy Roquemore (Mike Hopson, Jacksonville – 2nd)
1966 – Texas State Am – Hal Underwood (Del Rio)
1966 – Jacksonville – Sandy Haynes
1967 – Palestine -- Ras Allen (Dallas) (Leroy Roquemore – 2nd)
1968 – Nacogdoches – Wayne Gotcher (Houston) (Dean Wood, Liberty – 2nd)
1968 – Jacksonville – Tommy Cruse (Leroy Roquemore – 2nd)
1968 – Palestine – John Mahaffey (Kerrville) (Leroy Roquemore – 2nd)
1969 – Jacksonville – Tommy Cruse
1969 – Palestine – John Mahaffey (Frank Duphorne, Palestine – 2nd)
1970 – Palestine – James Marshall (Beaumont) (Dean Overturf – 2nd)
1970 – Jacksonville – Tommy Cruse (Mike Hopson – 2nd)
1971 – Jacksonville – Mike Hopson (Lloyd Hughes, Dallas – 2nd)
1972 – Jacksonville – Don Dacus (Jacksonville) (Leroy Roquemore – 2nd)
1973 – Nacogdoches – Tommy Tyson (Houston)
1973 – Jacksonville – Mark Triggs (Tyler) (Wade Cobb, Jacksonville – 2nd)
1974 – Nacogdoches – Tommy Tyson

Sources

Thirty Years of Championship Golf, Gene Sarazen, Prentice-Hall, Inc., New York, New York

Centennial, Curt Sampson, Brown Books Publishing Group, Dallas, Texas

Texas Golf Legends, Curt Sampson, Texas Tech University Press, Lubbock, Texas

Texas Golf Hall of Fame Website, Frances Trimble, San Antonio, Texas

The Tyler Morning Telegraph, Tyler, Texas

The Longview Journal, Longview, Texas

The Dallas Morning News, Dallas, Texas

The Odessa American, Odessa, Texas

The Register Herald, Beckley, West Virginia

CPSIA information can be obtained
at www.ICGtesting.com
Printed in the USA
FFOW04n1313190518
46703834-48802FF

9 780985 326340